WITHOUT EVIDENCE

The Rape of Justice in Wyoming

Jeane S. Wagner

Printed in the United States of America
at Pioneer Printing
Cheyenne, Wyoming

The cover photograph, two cartoons and the McArthur photograph are used, with appreciation, by express permission of the Casper Star Tribune, Casper, Wyoming.

The photograph of Dr. Story and his family is used by courtesy of the Story family.

ISBN 0-9624239-0-4

Library of Congress Catalog
Card Number 89-90442

Jeane S. Wagner
Post Office Box 5161, Cheyenne, Wyoming
82003

DEDICATED TO

DOC AND MARILYN, THE REAL VICTIMS

ACKNOWLEDGMENTS

I owe a great debt of gratitude to many people.

First to my husband, without whose unfailing help with every conceivable detail, I could never have finished the project,

To Jerod Story and Jan Hillman, who provided so much of the material I needed to document the book,

To my good friend, Arni Burron, who never let me get discouraged,

And finally, to the rest of my family, who helped when they could, and never got impatient with my preoccupation.

Countless others were there when I needed them and to all I say, inadequate though it may be, thank you!

I also wish to acknowledge with thanks the permission to use quotations from the Casper Star Tribune and the Dr. Story Defense Committee's newsletter, "The Real Story." I am also grateful for permission from the Story family to use the "Web of Relationships" as re-drawn for publication by C. E. Wagner.

Whenever dialogue appears within quotation marks, it represents an accurate transcription of testimony by trial participants, statements in pre-trial investigations or conversations carefully documented.

Some quotations are taken from taped live talk shows in Denver, Colorado and the "60 Minutes" segment aired in 1987.

INTRODUCTION

More than four years have passed since Dr. John Story, accused of raping female patients on his examining table, was convicted without sufficient evidence and sent to the Wyoming State Penitentiary.

There have been attorney after attorney, appeal after appeal and still no progress has been made toward his release.

In spite of a recent book written by a noted author which tries to erase any doubt that Dr. Story is guilty, the doctor's many friends and supporters across the nation continue in their unwavering opinion that the only rape committed was the rape of justice in Wyoming.

These supporters have been called "victims of Story, along with other good, intelligent folks."

That is hogwash. "Intelligent folks" who have studied the records, tracked down and exposed errors, inconsistencies, lies and prejudice, will not submit to such casual dismissal of their efforts and beliefs.

They are not a small group of locals who adored the town doctor - they are educated, dedicated people who, knowing both the accusers and the accused, cast their lot with the man who was apparently the victim of a plan to destroy him.

Many did so even though he was not their doctor, some did so in spite of long-standing disagreement with the doctor's religious and/or political views. Still others actually feel little for the doctor himself, but like the rest, deplore the circumstances under which an innocent man can be convicted of rape with no evidence except the word of one or more women.

It must be noted too, that these staunch supporters of Dr. Story's innocence are the area's most successful business people, prestigious public officials, professionals such as doctors, nurses, lawyers, accountants, pastors, teachers, journalists, and even more importantly, the men and women "on the street," representing nearly every occupation. Further, they are almost without exception, people of highest reputation in their communities.

In uniting against injustice, this nucleus of some eight hundred people in Wyoming's Big Horn Basin have managed to draw enough attention to the case that their numbers now include individuals and groups from California to Massachusetts. All have come offering help, their only commonality the determination to see justice done, not devotion to a person whom many of them have never met.

Certainly, the Dr. Story Defense Committee in Lovell was the original support group, but it has grown to proportions which cannot be ignored or ridiculed out of existence.

Having said this, it is necessary to acknowledge the difficulty of helping a convicted man. The law has said he is guilty, convicted by a jury of his peers, and backtracking from this position becomes harder with each new effort. Nevertheless, the case is still in litigation, with a new appeal before the Wyoming Supreme Court filed the seventh day of June 1989.

This book, based on the author's personal knowledge of the case and fully documented, seeks to help change the direction of the case by exposing critical actions and attitudes, out-of-court admissions and inconsistencies, and pre-trial changes in vital matters to make testimony more credible. Finally, it gives the public an opportunity to learn the "other side of the story."

Dr. John Story, in his correspondence from prison, has taken to adding a postscript to every letter that goes out.

He says, "I am not, nor have I ever been a rapist, nor do I invade anyone's personhood!"

Remember this as you read what must be told about the case that a constitutional lawyer calls a "judicial nightmare."

Wounds were inflicted in 1985 which will never heal - on a small-town doctor, his family and the entire community where he lived and practiced for twenty-six years.

Dr. John Story of Lovell, Wyoming, was convicted of raping or attempting to rape his female patients on the basis of "evidence" like this:

A forty-four-year-old woman stated under oath that Dr. Story assaulted her repeatedly in 1967. She then admitted returning to him and allowing her children to be treated by him until 1983.

The elderly widow of a policeman told the court that her physician of twenty years attempted to rape her in 1977. She deflected the effort, she said, then rose, dressed and paid her bill on the way out, saying nothing to anyone.

CHAPTER 1

Few experiences can induce the despair and loneliness of imprisonment. In the case of an innocent man, add the pain of betrayal and injustice, and existence becomes nearly unbearable. Yet Dr. John Huntington Story, convicted and now serving the third of a fifteen to twenty year sentence for crimes he, his family, friends, patients and colleagues say he did not commit, still has the utmost confidence in his God and his own intellect and integrity.

As he labors in the law library of the Wyoming State Penitentiary and meticulously prepares appeal after appeal as a part of his plan for "post conviction relief," this Christian doctor refers often to the time "when," not "if," he will be free.

At home in the tiny town of Lovell, Wyoming, an equally courageous woman suffers anguish more devastating than widowhood as she works and prays for the eventual exoneration and release of her husband. Marilyn Story, no less devout than the doctor, says and believes that God will not give her more than she can bear.

John and Marilyn Story, married for thirty years at the time he was accused of monstrous crimes against his patients, had always considered themselves an unremarkable couple. They were both the offspring of middle class parents, John from a background of small-town merchandising in Nebraska and Marilyn a ranch girl from the mountains of Colorado. Both of their childhood homes were steeped in traditional Christianity and the commitments they made early in life continued to strengthen them through adolescence and into adulthood.

John spent his first eighteen years in Maxwell, Nebraska, one of three children in the family. He served in the U.S. Navy during World War II, attended first Wheaton College in Wheaton, Illinois and then the University of Nebraska, where he received his degree in medicine. From graduation, he went to internship in Omaha, a residency in

Ogden, Utah, practiced for a year back in Nebraska and then, in 1958, moved with a wife and small daughter, to Lovell.

Marilyn Taussig had come into his life in 1953. They were married and she set about helping him build the career which was to prove successful and fulfilling to them both for thirty years.

Their marriage was at times hectic, with the pressures of a busy medical practice interfering with family activities, but their devotion to one another transcended petty difficulties and their home life reflected a deep contentment with their life together. Marital fidelity came naturally to them and they shared the desire for a family, so when their first child, Susan, arrived in 1955, she was joyfully received. A second daughter, Linda, was born four years later, and was also welcomed with thanksgiving.

When the decision was made to move to the remote northwestern part of Wyoming, it was because, as Dr. Story (now known to his friends as "Doc") said, "They (Lovell) had a real need."

This concern for the "real needs" of the world was to guide Doc through the next twenty-six years, even leading him to serve two medical missionary stints, one in Honduras in the late 60's and another in 1983. Ironically, both ended in tragedy, as a third daughter was killed in a neighborhood accident while he was away the first time and in 1983, he came home to find his name besmirched by women accusing him of rape.

The family's growing-up years were normal, happy ones. The girls did well in school, and along with their parents, took part in church and civic activities. Friendships were formed with people of like values and beliefs, and the Storys' social life consisted of the usual pastimes in small communities - evenings with friends, ball games, trips to the big city, weekend mountain trips, summer barbecues and holiday get-togethers.

As a family, they tried to take a real vacation each year away from the responsibilities of caring for patients, and in the early 70's visited Guatemala. There they met and befriended a teenage girl whose greatest ambition was to visit the United States. She later made her home with them for several months, learning the English language and the security of living in the circle of a warm, Christian family.

From 1958 to 1983 was a time of satisfying relationships between family members, patients, friends and casual acquaintances. The Storys lived quiet lives in a quiet neighborhood, accepted and esteemed as an integral part of the community. If Doc's strong conservative views and his tendency to "lecture" people on religion and politics sometimes grated on the nerves of those who held different opinions, it was overlooked in favor of his reputation as a fine doctor and a morally upright man.

Even early 1983 was good, when Doc was offered a second opportunity to serve on a medical mission, this time in Jamaica. With no children at home, Marilyn was able to join him and it was an enriching experience for them both.

Then it all ended. Today, "Doc" Story is in prison for allegedly raping his female patients during gynecological examinations, accused by nine women and skewered by a Wyoming law which says that **NO CORROBORATION** is necessary for conviction in sexual assault cases.

How could it happen? How, indeed.

CHAPTER 2

It wouldn't be fair to blame the town of Lovell itself for Doc and Marilyn Story's troubles, but the nature and composition of the community must be understood as a prelude to the rest of the story.

Lovell, Wyoming, population less than 2500, lies at the extreme northern end of a primarily agricultural "basin," formed by the Big Horn mountains on the east, the Absarokas on the west, the Pryors on the north, and the Owl Creek and Bridger mountains forming the southern lip. The chief crop for nearly 100 years has been sugar beets, grown most successfully by sturdy, stubborn German-Russian farmers, aided by an intricate irrigation system built by Mormon pioneers, who settled in the nearby Cowley area in 1900. Today the sugar market has fallen on hard times and Lovell's economy with it, but the factory still operates as Lovell's only enduring industry and its towering sugar bins hover protectively over the town.

Lovell is a neat, pretty little place, sometimes snow-covered from November till April, but capable of almost breathtaking beauty during the short spring and summer seasons. In the years when a late frost doesn't nip their fragile buds, lilacs bloom in profusion, filling warm nights with their fragrance. At either end of Main Street, there is a rose garden, lovingly tended by a town gardener and the source of Lovell's nickname, the "Rose Town." The riotous colors and sweet perfume of the roses attract bees, hummingbirds and a few tourists, although Lovell has never mastered the art of "tourism" as an industry. Smog is unheard of and sunshine and blue skies are taken for granted.

The business district consists of three blocks along both sides of Main, culminating in Lovell's focal point, the sprawling Stake House of the Church of Jesus Christ of Latter-Day Saints (Mormon), which dominates a full block of the town and nearly seventy percent of its residents. Catty-corner and slightly east of this imposing structure is the Lutheran (still known among old-timers as the "German-Lutheran") church, with its second-highest membership. Scattered out from there are Methodist, Baptist and Catholic churches, with a comparative newcomer, the Lovell Bible Church, sitting close to the town limits, but nevertheless very much a vital part of the community. It is to this group of witnessing Christians that the Story family belongs.

Outwardly, apart from its religious make-up, Lovell (until the Dr. Story episode) was much like any other small town in Wyoming. On a pleasant summer evening, with the scent of freshly mown grass in the air and the sound of laughter as neighbors visited after a backyard barbecue, it would have been hard to believe the events could happen which destroyed friendships, polarized families and caused the boycott of businesses. But happen they did, and now the atmosphere of the whole town is tainted by the knowledge that one of its leading citizens is in prison, unjustly so, according to a large percentage of residents.

"It's like something dark and heavy hanging over us," Bev Moody, one of the doctor's strongest supporters, says, her brown eyes clouded as she looks around her once-thriving floral shop. "My husband and I have always lived here and this business was a dream come true for me, but the way things are now, we wonder if we should have left long ago."

Lovell was never a boom town, in spite of nearby Big Horn National Recreation Area, which some residents hoped would bring prosperity in the '70's. It has been "depressed" before, but never like it is now. As many buildings along Main street are vacant as occupied, and the remaining businesses are fighting for survival. North Big Horn Hospital, once bustling with activity, by 1987 had fallen to a shocking 24.7 percent occupancy.

A local businessman and life-long booster of his hometown, explains it ruefully. "I guess we were too complacent for too long," he says, "Lovell had always survived without much outside influence and we thought it always would, but this thing has about got us down for the count."

"This thing" of course, is the monumental controversy generated by Dr. Story's conviction, which continues to be a source of fierce conflict between those who say he is guilty and his supporters, who claim he was "sand-bagged.

"The tongue is like a fire..it sets on fire the entire course of our existence with the fire that comes to it from hell itself...No man has been able to tame the tongue. It is evil and uncontrollable, full of deadly poison." James 3:5-6

CHAPTER 3

Despite the consequences, it is in the official record that the Story matter began with rumors, and as his pastor, Rev. Ken Buttermore, said later, "Doc was not nearly as outraged by the accusations against him as most men would be."

Normally of a passive nature, Doc said he was sorry people would say such things about him, but otherwise, he continued to practice medicine and at least outwardly, hardly acknowledged that there was a problem.

To understand this casual attitude toward such serious charges, one needs to have lived in Lovell, where rumors constantly abound and the old adage, "where there's smoke there's fire," doesn't necessarily apply.

One former resident describes Lovell as a "rumor mill," and says, "All small towns are gossip-ridden, but in Lovell it's more than a pastime, it's a way of life."

The Storys had been subjected to gossip before - nothing so vicious as this, but rumors nevertheless, which unfortunately contributed to their feeling that, while disturbing and depressing, this too would pass and be forgotten.

One rumor had not been forgotten, but it was more of a source of amusement than distress. A few years after they arrived in Lovell, the rumor circulated that Marilyn's father had died and left her several million dollars. Actually, her father was in good health at the time and his death was some ten years later. Too, while he was a retired rancher with means to make life comfortable for himself and his wife in their remaining years, the idea of his bequeathing millions of dollars to Marilyn, only one of several children, was laughable. In spite of the Storys' modest lifestyle, this bit of gossip persisted, and would surface from time to time over the years.

Marilyn, while seemingly more upset than the doctor over the sexual accusations against him, had complete faith and trust in her husband and the thought that there was any truth to the rumors never crossed her mind.

Another woman, herself a patient of the doctor's and mother of one of his employees, expressed similar confidence in him. "It never bothered me for one minute to have my daughter working for him," she said, "because I didn't believe any of it. It's totally ludicrous."

Ludicrous, ridiculous, bizarre. Those and other words of disbelief were to dominate many conversations as the fire of rumor spread, consuming everything in its path.

CHAPTER 4

It all began on a fine day in May, 1983, when Dean and Arden McArthur, Mormon parents of nine children, dropped a bombshell on their hometown. For openers, they called on Cal Taggart, who had served Big Horn County for eleven years as state senator. Cal had always encouraged his constituents to bring their questions, problems and complaints to him and they did, but this was the strangest story he had ever heard.

The McArthurs' two married daughters, Meg Anderson and Minda Brinkerhoff, they said, had been "violated" by Dr. Story during pelvic examinations in years past. Cal was aghast. His office was the public relations center of the Big Horn Basin - nothing escaped his notice, particularly anything which was potentially harmful to his hometown of Lovell.

Furthermore, Dr. Story had been Cal's family physician for nearly twenty years and they knew him to be a competent, compassionate man. His honor and integrity were indisputable and the idea of such sordid behavior was completely out of character. No one had ever heard Doc use profanity or obscenity and his manners with women bordered on old-worldliness. His wife, Marilyn, a petite brunette with a quiet charm, helped in the doctor's office, worked in school and church organizations and took an active part in the Lovell Woman's Club. Her eyes sometimes reflected the pain of losing an eighteen-month-old daughter in a tragic accident, but otherwise she was a typical contented wife and mother. The couple's two daughters, Susan and Linda, both now grown and away from home, were bright, pretty girls, well-adjusted and devoted to their parents and each other. Susan, the older, had also helped in the doctor's office as a teenager, and later as a registered nurse until the lure of new experiences and a larger town took her away. (Illustration)

Cal tried to elicit more information from the McArthurs. Why hadn't they reported the incidents sooner and why to him instead of the police? This seemed particularly curious, since Meg's husband, Danny, was a Lovell policeman and Minda's husband, Scott, had an uncle who was a state investigator. Scott was also related to several employees of the Lovell police department.

Why had the entire family continued to go to Dr. Story after the alleged attacks? Why had Meg and Minda continued to take their children to him?

The answers were vague, but the assertions remained strong. Dean and Arden insisted that Dr. Story was a rapist.

What were they going to do about it? The McArthurs told Cal that their daughters had already written letters of complaint to the State Board of Medical Examiners in Cheyenne and were awaiting a response.

Cal sat at his desk for a long time after the McArthurs left. He knew that Doc was innocent, and besides, the accusations

Doc, Marilyn, Susan and Linda
in happier days

made no sense at all, but what on earth could motivate people to bring such charges? Finally, he called his wife. Irene, a tiny, vivacious woman, exploded in his ear. "They're lying," she said flatly.

That evening, Cal and Irene discussed the matter at length. Between husband and wife, the simple logistics were carefully considered as they would be in nearly every home in Lovell as the case progressed. That a small man, 5'6", would have difficulty maneuvering himself into a position from which he could have intercourse with a woman on his examining table without her knowing in advance what his intentions were, seemed obvious. According to Arden and Dean, their daughters had not experienced any touching, fondling, suggestive conversation, or even a leer to alert them to danger. Neither had they been restrained in any way. The assaults, they said, had been accomplished with the doctor standing at the foot of the table, while his "victims" were in the classic gynecological position, unable to see anything but their own draped knees.*

Moreover, the "violations" had taken place, Arden said, not once, but several times. At first her daughters only "suspected" that they had been raped, and so continued to make and keep appointments with Dr. Story. That two married women over the age of twenty-five would be in doubt about whether they had been raped or not, and further would continue to go to the doctor whom they "thought" was assaulting them, the Taggarts agreed, was absurd. That opinion was shared by nearly everyone as the "Story story" spread like rancid butter over the town.

* Meg said in a later interview with Lovell Chief of Police Dave Wilcock, that she was mistaken in her first contact with the medical board when she told them she "saw his hips moving back and forth." It couldn't have been "actual sight," she said, "because I couldn't see."

CHAPTER 5

News travels fast in small towns and by noon of the next day, knots of people were gathering at the Rose Bowl and Dude's Cafe to share the latest gossip. The split which exists to this day had begun - In Lovell, you are for Dr. Story or against Dr. Story. Very few claim neutrality.

Although most of the doctor's accusers are Mormon, the division is not along religious lines. Given the large majority of Mormons in Lovell, the doctor probably has as many LDS supporters as others, and to them, the fault lies in the individuals, not the Church. In other words, if there was a "Mormon connection," it stemmed not from the hierarchy, but from an influential woman who seemingly used her authority in the church to draw others to her way of thinking.

History may clarify this point, but from the beginning, the news media referred frequently to Dr. Story's having "founded" the Lovell Bible Church, which he did not. It was also implied that most of the people who believed in his innocence were members of that group.

"What they seemed determined to do," says Jan Hillman, an intelligent, attractive young woman who has worked diligently in the doctor's behalf since the beginning, "was to create a 'Jim Jones' image, which is ridiculous."

"In the first place," she says, "we represent a wide variety of religious positions, from fundamental Christianity to nothing at all."

Indeed, the common denominator among Dr. Story's supporters is not religion, but the powerful desire to see justice done.

Wes Meeker, prominent realtor in the Big Horn Basin, and Doc's next-door neighbor, expresses this view.

"I'm anything but a follower of Doc's," he says whenever the subject comes up. "We're neighbors, but he's not my doctor and I guess you couldn't even say we're friends. The reason I'm working for his defense is that I know he's innocent and it's not only to see him vindicated, but to try to keep this kind of thing from happening to some other poor guy." *

Every man in the area is acutely aware of this possibility. Rex Nebel, former sheriff's deputy, said in a letter to the Casper Star-Tribune, "Right now a couple of women can file charges on a man in Big Horn county for the crime of rape and send him up with no physical evidence whatsoever! We better fight this kind of garbage while there's still time."

As Doc and Marilyn's plight became known around the country, mail received by the Dr. Story Defense Committee, headed by Jan and Wes, has included such comments as, "I plan to stay away from a state that hands every woman in it a loaded gun!"

In Lovell, disbelief in the doctor's guilt has always predominated. No poll has ever been taken, but according to a statement of support for him circulated immediately after the conviction, eight hundred adults were willing to be counted on his side.

In spite of the gravity of the situation, most of Dr. Story's women patients and employees laughed incredulously at the mere thought of any impropriety on his part. Dr. Story? No way! He would never even make an off-color remark, much less a pass at any woman. Diana Harrison, a secretary in the doctor's office said, "I felt that if I was hanging from a chandelier with a bikini on, he wouldn't notice." Diana later turned on her former employer and friend and testified against him at his criminal trial, offering some of the most bizarre and damaging testimony of all.

But by far the most widely discussed element of the whole matter was not Dr. Story, but his accusers, the McArthurs.

"As shocked as I was when I heard it," Kay Meeker, long-time patient and friend of the Story family, said, "I wasn't surprised by the source."

Her opinion was echoed in Cheyenne, Wyoming's capital city, where Sen. Taggart's former secretary reacted with, "So Arden's at it again!."

* Neither Jan Hillman or Wes Meeker are members of the Lovell Bible Church.

CHAPTER 6

The references to Arden McArthur's propensity for trouble-making were not surprising. Tall, sharp-featured and with a determined set to her jaw, she had a reputation for being a vindictive woman, strong-willed and influential. At home, she was believed to "rule the roost," and her daughters' testimony throughout the Story case reflected the domination of their mother in their lives. (Illustration)

At the time of the accusations against Dr. Story, Arden held a position in her church which gave her access to the minds of a large percentage of Lovell's female population. Her title was "President of Relief Society," which made her the counterpart of the Bishop, or having a mother-type authority over "all the sisters," both members and non-members of the LDS church.

Following the revocation of Dr. Story's medical license, the first step in his slide to disaster, people took to their typewriters and letters poured in to Senator Taggart, state authorities and the local newspaper. Arden McArthur's name appeared time after time. One said bluntly, "Dr. Story is not the first professional man to be attacked by Arden McArthur and her cohorts."

Star-Tribune/Linda Bean

Arden and Dean McArthur
December 2, 1984

Others blamed her without mentioning names. "This man (Dr. Story) has been wrongfully accused, and his life's reputation ruined by a person who is always involved in some similar situation, whether it be a teacher in the Lovell schools or a state highway patrolman she didn't like."

The other "professional man" was Dean Gerke, a high school teacher and coach, who upon hearing of the accusations against Dr. Story, directed an open letter to the people of Lovell by way of the Lovell Chronicle, the town's weekly newspaper.

"As many of you know," he wrote from his home in Montana, "we too, were subject to insinuations, falsehoods, phone campaigns and secret meetings which led to our moving away from Lovell. We chose not to fight the issue - it is very difficult to prevail against this type of attack.

"But maybe we should have chosen a different route. Perhaps the time has come for us all to fight back against this terrible injustice taking place in Doc and Marilyn's lives. We would like to urge each of you to support Dr. Story in any way you can. And to you people who are responsible for this, shame on you! What a loss Dr. Story would be to your community!"

Mr. Gerke, not a member of the Bible Church, did not specifically name his adversary, but former hospital administrator Joe Brown, did. He put in words what nearly every citizen of Lovell knew, that Mr. Gerke had taught a human sexuality course in school and when Minda McArthur got pregnant by her boyfriend, Scott, whom she later married, Arden blamed it on the popular teacher and his choice of instructional material. Following a barrage of rumors and gossip, Coach Gerke and his family decided to leave Lovell.

While the town seethed and boiled, the accusers doggedly continued the persecution they had started. Meg Anderson, almost wraith-like with her long white hair and light eyes, and the more flamboyant, reddish blonde Minda Brinkerhoff, were both flighty and giggly at ages twenty-six and twenty-seven. In addition to writing poorly spelled, disjointed letters to the Board of Medical Examiners, they told long, rambling stories of their experiences with Dr. Story. Their basic contention was that he had "dilated them with his penis," but their accounts were generously interspersed with such expressions as, "I thought," "I suspected," "it felt like" and "he seemed to be." They told of going back to Dr. Story several times after their first suspicions, and even after they decided they had actually been raped, continuing to take their children to him because "he was the only doctor I trusted," one said, and the other declared, "I loved the man." They were snubbed by some and ridiculed by others, while the more charitable pitied them for presumed emotional instability.

Dean McArthur, less aggressive than his wife, had by now retreated from the front lines, and began to have second thoughts about the controversy he and his wife had stirred up, but his daughters and Arden had gone too far to turn back.

For one thing, Arden was now claiming to have had a very interesting religious experience. Some time late in June, she said, she had taken a group of Mormon young people to Idaho Falls, Idaho on a "temple excursion." These trips serve the purpose of baptizing the youth of the church for the dead, and are well-chaperoned by parents and other adults.

On this particular excursion, Arden said later, she was seated in the chapel while the others were "doing baptism for the dead," when she was **levitated** out of her chair. "I went to the matron," she said, "and asked for the prayer roll and she directed me to it. Then I wrote just as fast as I could and I put Dr. Story's name and Marilyn's name, his children's names, my family's name, anybody that I could think (of) that was directly involved, on the prayer roll."*

Apparently, Arden took this as a sign from her Heavenly Father that she should continue vigorously with the crusade she had begun against Dr. Story and when she returned to Lovell, she began contacting women on the street, by telephone and through Relief Society, asking them if they had ever had any bad experience with the doctor. Those who "thought they might have," were urged to write letters of complaint to the Board of Medical Examiners.

Much later, after Dr. Story's conviction as a rapist, the Lovell police chief was quoted in the state's largest daily newspaper, the Casper Star-Tribune, as saying the investigation started with the names of twelve women who "according to **gossip**, might have a complaint against Story."

He further admitted, "They (rumors) had no substance - some of them were just a murmur in a cafe."

Without evidence of any kind, only

rumors and gossip, the Lovell Police Department began contacting women and a case was built which placed a man's reputation, and finally his life, in jeopardy.

* There seems to be a difference of opinion among Mormons about the validity of levitation as a religious experience. Some think it is evil and one former Lovellite now living elsewhere in Wyoming, suggested that if Arden said it happened to her in the temple, she should be reprimanded by the church.

CHAPTER 7

Why would a woman who professed to "cherish" Dr. Story, his wife and children, who had demonstrated that fondness through the years with gifts and loving attention, make such a complete about-face? If her daughters had been legitimate victims of rape by the doctor, Arden McArthur would have been justified in bringing about his arrest and conviction, but their flimsy stories simply did not stand up under scrutiny, a fact apparently recognized by County Prosecuting Attorney Terrill Tharp when he put together the criminal case against Dr. Story. Meg and Minda's accusations were not included, because, he said, "they would hurt the case."

Many months later, after Doc's conviction, Oprah Winfrey, Chicago talk-show hostess, interviewed Meg and Minda along with several other accusers and referred to them as "the ones who started all this." Viewers who knew the two Lovell women were astonished to hear Minda say, "I hate to hear you say that," when in fact, both she and Meg had been irate when their charges were dismissed by County Attorney Tharp. "It is like a slap in the face," they told a Casper Star Tribune reporter in March 1985.

Almost everyone in Lovell speculated on

Arden's change of heart toward the Story family. Granted, there were reasons for her to be hurt and angry with Dr. Story at times, but hardly more than could occur in any friendship.

For instance, the relationship cooled noticeably in 1982, when Doc refused to certify a document declaring Dean eligible for a disability allowance from the state. Dean had suffered a heart attack and following specialized treatment and surgery in Billings, Montana, Arden brought the form to Doc, who to her dismay, declined to sign it. Actually, according to Marilyn, even if Doc had felt that Dean was permanently disabled, he would not have been able to sign the form. "That was the responsibility of the cardiologist on the case," Marilyn recalls, "as Doc had not done the surgery or really had anything to do with it except some post-operative care. Arden kept calling us about it, saying she couldn't get through to the Billings doctor, or he was gone, or some other excuse, but Doc was adamant and never did sign."

"Was Arden unhappy or upset over that?"

"Very much. Things were never quite the same again," Marilyn said.

Also, the care and maintenance of a family of eleven takes constant penny-watching unless you are independently wealthy, which the McArthurs were not. In fact, early in the investigation, a Mormon lady of long acquaintance with the McArthur family, said what was well known in Lovell.

"I never knew them when they didn't have a get-rich-quick scheme going," she said. "Once they had a knitting mill they were going to put in everyone's home and everyone was going to make a million." Another time, she said, it was hay equipment that they were going to make a fortune on.

Consequently, over the years, Dr. Story's bill for medical attention to the whole family, grew and grew, until by 1983 it had reached unmanageable proportions. Arden did the doctor's office laundry, but this hardly made a dent in the overall obligation. Doc and Marilyn recall that at one time, the McArthurs had offered land in lieu of cash. Since the property was suitable neither for the new clinic Doc planned to build or a proposed hospital addition, he disappointed Arden again by refusing to take the land himself or influence the hospital board to buy it.

Minda and her husband, Scott, had also run up a sizable bill, and on being confronted with their accusations against him, Dr. Story said (in one of the few impulsive moments of his life) that if they felt he had mistreated Minda in any way, they could forget the bill.

This was construed by his detractors as an admission of guilt, which of course was not the case. It was simply an unwise attempt to show them how outrageous he considered their claims, born of the anger and hurt he kept buried so successfully most of the time.

Minda said in an investigative interview following the medical board hearing that her first suspicion that Dr. Story was assaulting her came in 1980, over three years before she and her husband approached Dr. Story about it. No wonder the doctor reacted as he did.

I was revolted," he said later, "I just

wanted them out of my office and out of my life."

The final straw which caused the close relationship between two families to collapse, may have been Arden's acute disappointment in her own failure to convert the Storys to her faith. She and the doctor had discussed religion constantly over the years they had been acquainted, he trying to educate her in the Judeo-Christian ethic and she hoping to bring him and his family into the Mormon fold.

Arden was not hesitant about saying she would "give anything" if her doctor held a priesthood in the Mormon church, because it would give her more "power, trust and faith."*

"That expression baffled us," Marilyn says now, "we couldn't imagine the desire for personal power being a reason for proselyting."

None of these resentments should justify the kind of action Arden seemed to be promoting against Dr. Story, but who knows the mind and spirit of an angry and disappointed woman?

* Not unexpectedly, Arden denied in July 1985 when she was interviewed by Joan Barron of the Casper Star-Tribune, that she ever asked Dr. Story to join the Mormon church. "I only want good people to join my church," she said.

CHAPTER 8

In November 1984, eighteen months after the original accusations by the McArthurs, some of Lovell's residents felt they had the answer to why the whole thing had happened. Meg and Minda filed civil suits against Dr. Story totalling three million dollars. Acccording to a news report in the Northern Wyoming Daily News, Meg's suit alleged that Dr. Story had sexual intercourse with her "on or about November 15, 1982, and **at various times preceding that date."** She was asking for $500,000 in actual damages and $1,000,000 in punitive damages. (Emphasis added)

Minda alleged that the doctor had sexual intercourse "**without her knowledge or consent** on April 21, 1983, and **at other times** in Story's medical office." (emphasis added) She also asked for $500,000 in actual damages and $1,000,000 in punitive damages.

It was not explained how a woman could sue a man for rape that she didn't recognize as such until months or years later.

This action followed closely on the heels of the doctor's arrest and to some was completely incomprehensible, while others nodded their heads wisely and said it "figured" that the McArthurs had money in mind when they started the trouble.

Through his attorney, Dr. Story quickly filed a countersuit against the two for $10,000,000, claiming that they intentionally inflicted "emotional distress" on him by filing their lawsuits. He also alleged the women slandered him and interfered with his business. (Illustration)

Speculation ran high, as McArthur detractors mulled over how far $3,000,000 would go, even split several ways.

This might have been a reasonable assumption, except for the fact that the McArthurs and their attorneys surely knew the doctor's finances would be drained by the expense of defending himself in criminal court. Unless, of course, the old rumor that Marilyn had squirreled away several million dollars was still alive and well!*

Whatever the reason, the McArthurs gladly settled out of court for $3,000 shortly after Dr. Story's conviction, much to the chagrin of many of the doctor's supporters, but as the defense committee said, "He reluctantly paid this so he could limit his battle to the appeal."

*This may well have been the case in light of Meg Anderson's comment later that their lawyers had been unable to locate the Story's money.

A12—Star-Tribune, Casper, Wyo. Thursday, Dec. 6, 1984

A cartoonist's view of lawsuits and countersuit

CHAPTER 9

Doc and Marilyn Story, like all medical people, knew of the tendency for some women patients to fantasize about their doctors, and this was considered a plausible reason for stories of imagined sexual encounters to get started.

The same clinical psychologist who examined Dr. Story and then voluntarily offered his comments on the case, spoke specifically of this possibility.

"It is a well known phenomenon that women tend to have love/sexual fantasies about their physicians, especially when obstetrical and gynecological issues are involved. The discussions among women on this issue are common and it is my understanding that the medical community is well aware of it. This issue could be a powerful dynamic which might be the core fantasy around which a myth is built.

"Persons who are sexually frustrated or have marriages that are not working well would be prime candidates for an excessive fantasy life around sexual-medical procedures."

Unfortunately, Doc, throughout his career, had chosen to ignore the possibility of any real harm coming to him from such delusions, and had steadfastly resisted having a third party in the examining room with him. In the 50's, when medicine became very "defensive," as a fellow physician, Dr. Douglas Wrung, also of Lovell, described it, more and more doctors felt the need to protect themselves by having a nurse present during gynecological examinations. No law was passed to this effect in Wyoming, however, and it was left to the doctors themselves to take this precaution.

Kay Meeker was one of those who stated firmly that she preferred not to have another woman in the room. "In a town the size of Lovell," she said, "the doctor's nurse could be your best friend, or your neighbor, and that would be too embarrassing." Nita Bronkema, a registered nurse who worked in Doc's office, concurred with a smile. "I remember that after I prepared one lady, the doctor asked her if she wanted me to stay, and she said, 'it's not that I don't like you, Nita, but I'll really feel more comfortable without you here.'"

Another patient said it differently. "Dr. Story was a physician of the old school. He firmly believed that as a doctor under the Hippocratic oath, he was to be trusted, and in turn, he trusted his patients. He was determined to keep the doctor-patient relationship completely confidential and those of us who had no problems at home or in our own minds, never questioned the practice."

That sounds naive now, and indeed, naiveté has been mentioned as a reason for Doc's attitude.

With new female patients, Dr. Story did make the concession of asking if they wanted a nurse in the room. "I told him 'no,'" one said, "because I feel very vulnerable with a nurse in there." Others said they either preferred not to have one or that it made no difference to them, thus reinforcing his belief that he had nothing to fear.

The other reason for his opposition to what had become standard procedure with most doctors was another facet of Doc's personality. Fiercely independent and at loggerheads with many of Wyoming's physicians politically and philosophically, he deeply resented anything which he perceived to be interference in his private decisions. Therefore, when subjects came up pertaining to individual practice, he simply refused to listen or be influenced by his peers. After all, he knew his patients and he would conduct his business as he saw fit, not as dictated to him by others, no matter how well-intentioned.

Dr. Story's friends, even understanding and possibly agreeing with his reasons, are the first to admit that not having a nurse in the room during gynecological exams was bad judgment, but as his defense counsel said, "to take that bit of information and stretch it to a conclusion...that because he didn't have a third person in there somehow equates to guilt, is, in my opinion, absurd. That's a big leap."

Although Doc says now that his days in Lovell before the trouble began were the happiest of his life, he must surely acknowledge to himself in the cold loneliness of his prison cell, that it might all have been avoided if he had compromised just a little. But "compromise" is a word not to be found in Dr. John Story's vocabulary.

CHAPTER 10

In due time, Meg and Minda's letters to the Board of Medical Examiners were considered, and Dr. Story was summoned to Cheyenne to defend himself.

David Garner, long-time friend of the Story family reflects, "Doc probably didn't do himself any good at that time. He's completely honest with himself and others, and it just never occurred to him that if he told the truth he wouldn't be believed. Feeling as he did about having to answer to such charges, I'm sure his manner was anything but conciliatory."

"As a matter of fact," he continues, "none of us were too worried yet. We were confident that he was innocent and we still had faith in the justice system. We had a lot to learn!"

In spite of the doctor's flat denial of any wrongdoing, the board members felt they needed to pursue the matter further. They advised him to seek legal counsel and prepare for the matter to be decided at a formal hearing. His younger daughter, Linda, explains what happened next.

"In August 1983, Dad retained a Cody (Wyoming) lawyer, Mr. Charles Kepler, to represent him at the formal hearing. Still thinking the absurdity of the charges would be obvious to the doctors hearing the case, a low-key defense was prepared."

"'Low-key' has been one of the biggest mistakes consistently made in this whole case," David continues, "but at that time, no one could foresee what was still coming."

The medical board hearing didn't take place until the next spring (1984) and during the intervening seven months, Dr. Story and Marilyn put it all in God's hands and he continued to practice in Lovell, with some decrease in patient load, but still plenty of work to keep him occupied.

On the periphery of his wide base of support, though, the rumors had been gaining momentum. Four more women claimed to have experienced "improprieties" in the past, and were included on the list of witnesses to appear at the medical board hearing.

One of them, Aletha Durtsche, caused already straining eyebrows to go even higher. Aletha, a married woman with three children, often spoke about men making improper advances to her.

She was, and still is, a mail delivery woman and one of her co-workers at the post office reacted to the news that Aletha claimed to have been assaulted by Dr. Story with indignation.

"I don't know when she says this happened," she said, her eyes snapping angrily, "but if it was more than ten minutes ago, it isn't true, because she can't keep a secret any longer than that!"

Actually, Aletha had never reported any improprieties by Dr. Story. She only agreed to file a complaint when contacted by Arden McArthur, a fact she admitted freely in court and again on two TV programs.

According to friends, acquaintances and even her Avon lady, Aletha was always very "frank" in the things she told them - "nothing is too private."

"We knew about her sex life with her husband, what kind of birth control they used, what he said and did to her and when they had any problems at home, we heard a lot more than we really wanted to know," one said.

Aletha also spoke freely about men on her mail route who made "insinuating remarks" and "tried to move in on her" and once in a Relief Society meeting said she had been molested as a child.

One person described her as "insecure," and having a need to "always be the smartest and best in everything."

With this background, surely Aletha would not be an effective witness against Dr. Story, his supporters told themselves.

The medical board hearing was held in March 1984 in Worland, Wyoming and was a private, confidential proceeding, involving four of the five-member board, their lawyer, Kathleen Karpan to represent the six complainants, Dr. Story and his attorney and retired Judge John Raper as hearing officer. The transcripts of this hearing were sealed shortly after its close and no testimony from it could be used either in the criminal trial or to explain the action of the board members. Of the six accusers however, Aletha Durtsche was the only one whose case went to criminal court, so it is to be presumed that the charges of the other five were even less credible than hers. Excerpts from Aletha's testimony at the criminal trial will be explored later to show the kind of "evidence" on which a man's fate was decided.

Marilyn Story distinctly remembers the feeling of optimism she had after the hearing when her husband's attorney told her he believed they had won the case and that Kathy Karpan, the lawyer for the other side, had said something to the same effect.*

The Board then had sixty days to review the evidence and arrive at a decision.

Those two months passed quickly, even for Doc and Marilyn, who continued to pray unceasingly and, as much as possible, maintain their normal lifestyle.

On June 7, however, to the surprise and dismay of Dr. Story and his supporters, the Board ruled to revoke his license to practice medicine, effective July 1, 1984. Bill Simpson, Attorney Kepler's partner and assistant on the case, said later of the decision, "We could only surmise that given the number of accusers and the seriousness of the charges, the doctors on the Board felt some action should be taken and revocation of his license was the only avenue open to them. I was then and still am, completely confident of Dr. Story's innocence."

Linda takes up the narrative again.

"Mr. Kepler immediately sought appeal of the revocation which would be decided by District Judge John T. Dixon," she says, "and was pleased that Judge Dixon stayed the revocation, allowing Dad to continue his medical practice during the appeal process.

"A tremendous amount of public outrage over the revocation and support for Dad was demonstrated when the Board's decision was handed down," Linda continues. "As a family, we were stunned. We knew then that Dad was in real trouble and we were floundering in an environment completely foreign to us."

More letters expressing confidence in Dr. Story and pleading with the Board to reconsider their decision, flooded the office of the medical board doctors and their executive secretary, Dr. Lawrence Cohen. Again, they came from professional colleagues, patients, friends and even people who were not personally involved with Dr. Story, but who knew the accusers and their reputations. Many were copied to other public officials, the attorney general of Wyoming and even the governor, but the only result was a dead silence from Cheyenne.

To the Story supporters who thought it obvious that the doctor was being railroaded, it was almost unbearably frustrating that no one seemed to care, at least no one with the power to do anything about it.

*Kathy Karpan, at that time an assistant to the Attorney General, resigned in early 1986 to pursue a career in politics. After an arduous campaign, she won the position of Secretary of State, which in Wyoming is the equivalent of Lieutenant Governor, or second in command of the state. Shortly after her election, at a gathering of career women, she said in an autobiographical sketch that during her time as attorney for the medical board, she had been instrumental in achieving the revocation of two medical licenses (one Dr. Story's).

CHAPTER 11

As a matter of fact, there is reason to believe that there were people who could have done something about it, but didn't want to.

Wayne Aarestad, a North Dakota attorney who entered the case in September 1984, after Mr. Kepler bowed out, saying he didn't want to be tied up in an increasingly lengthy and complex court battle, went to work immediately on the appeal to the Board of Medical Examiners.

It wasn't difficult to determine that Dr. Lawrence Cohen, Administrator of the Division of Public Health and Medical Services and Dr. Story had a long record of antipathy toward one another. It was known that Dr. Cohen had referred to Dr. Story as "incompetent" and refused to support a physician's assistance program in Lovell because of Dr. Story's presence there. The two had clashed on numerous occasions in the past twenty years over medical and political philosophy and hospital administration. An underlying personality conflict didn't help matters either.

It was also known that Dr. Cohen, in his capacity as Executive Secretary of the Board of Medical Examiners at that time, was the initiator of the proceedings against Dr.

Story and had played a large role in the selection and appointment of the current board members.*

It was also learned from Lovell residents who had been interviewed by a state investigator in the early stages of the Dr. Story case, that he (investigator) refused to accept any positive information about Dr. Story, and was insulting and intimidating to many of the witnesses who indicated there was no substance to the charges against the doctor.

The fact that the Board scheduled, then cancelled, all polygraph exams for Meg and Minda McArthur was also discovered and noted for future use.

It is a complex case. Frustrated women, rumors, gossip, allegedly prejudiced investigators and finally a decision-making body which might have gone into the hearing with preconceived impressions of Dr. Story's character and competence - all play their part.

* * *

UPDATE: According to Dr. Story's latest appeal to the Supreme Court, an offer was made to him which he did not accept.

"Before any charges were filed against Dr. Story, he was told by Kathy Karpan (then an Assistant Attorney General, now Secretary of State) that if he would simply leave Wyoming there would be no charges," the document reads.

The doctor says now from prison, that he refused that offer on the grounds that he was an innocent man, and he wanted the opportunity to have his name cleared in a court of law.

The decision was unanimous in the family. No one wanted to spend the rest of their days under a cloud and they felt sure he would be vindicated.

After the filing of the appeal Kathy Karpan denied, "unequivocally," that she ever made such an offer to Dr. Story.

"I was," she said, "never in a position to make that offer," and further, "that would have been up to the County Prosecuting Attorney."

The Secretary of State did say however, that she could not answer for anything Dr. Lawrence Cohen, Executive Secretary to the Board of Medical Examiners, might have done.

Dr. Cohen is deceased.

* Dr. Lawrence Cohen died in January 1988 after a long illness. He was highly respected in his native city of Cheyenne, having been in private practice for many years as a pediatrician. In 1967, he accepted a state appointment as Director of the Wyoming Department of Health and Social Services and served in that capacity under two governors.

CHAPTER 12

Following the revocation of his license, even though the action had been stayed and an appeal was being prepared, it was a subdued Dr. Story who continued "business as usual" in his hilltop clinic.

With the state board of medical examiners' decision going against him, he had to accept the fact that getting out of the predicament he was in would require more than trust in the judicial system. His faith in God never wavered and he and Marilyn often assured their supporters that they were "at peace" in spite of their difficulties. They were calm, concerned about others, and their demeanor was inspirational to their fellow Christians.

Members of the Lovell Bible Church organized regular prayer meetings in their behalf and the Bible lay open constantly for reference to passages concerning courage and forbearance.

Despite their great trust, though, the doctor and his family wanted desperately to believe that the next legal action would bring relief from the nightmare they were in, but as the days went by, they continued to hear of more women who were accusing him of sexual assault.

Again, letters written defending Doc's

innocence and sent to every conceivable authority, included references to the character and reputation of the women involved. And for the first time, it was suggested by several writers that such accusations can be incited.

"Every community, it seems, has its individuals who get satisfaction from stirring up trouble and **inciting** easily led, lonely and frustrated people into doing and saying things they normally wouldn't say or do," a co-worker of twelve years experience with the doctor and life-long acquaintance with his accusers wrote, and another, equally well-informed, agreed.

"It's hard to believe that of all the women who claim they were assaulted, not one came forward and made a complaint until **incited to do so!**"

A Methodist minister, no longer serving in Lovell, but still concerned for its welfare, described Dr. Story as "a man of deep commitment to his family, his profession and his faith," in a lengthy letter to the Lovell Chronicle.

In part, he said, "I am not calling any of the ladies involved liars. What I am saying is that they are confused between fact and fiction and also are being used by some who know how to manipulate and mold fiction into supposed fact."

This widely held belief was confirmed by a Denver, Colorado clinical psychologist, Dr. James Dolby, who examined Dr. Story in September 1984, at the request of the doctor's new attorney, Wayne Aarestad.

"There are many aspects of this case that remind me of the compounding delusional systems built upon some basic truths taken out of context," Dr. Dolby said in an addendum to his diagnostic conclusions.

"The Salem witchcraft trials are major examples," he said.

He further stated, "It is my opinion that if Dr. Story is not exonerated, it will indeed be a travesty of justice."

Dr. Dolby's official statement summing up the results of the interview and psychological testing was short and to the point.

"It is my professional opinion that Dr. Story is emotionally stable and suffers from no mental disturbance. The allegations of sexual abuse while functioning as a practicing physician are inconsistent with the results of this diagnostic examination."

Although this examination, along with a lie detector test which showed Dr. Story to be "truthful in regard to the allegations" and found "no deception indicated," were not used in his defense in court, Dr. Story has whatever comfort may be drawn from the opinions of experts.

Mr. Aarestad also did careful research into the background of the women accusing Dr. Story of sexual improprieties and made some interesting discoveries. Several had serious problems with delusions, fantasy and transference, along with histories of incest, venereal disease and abuse by parents and/or husbands.

The lawyer planned to base a major part of the appeal on the credibility and psychological profiles of the women, and to the relief of the doctor's wife and daughters, Dr. Story finally agreed.

"Up to that point, he had been reluctant to use such information against women who had been his patients," his younger daughter said, shaking her head as she often did over the years at some of her father's "hard-nosed" attitudes, "but his career and reputation had already suffered almost irreparable damage."

As it turned out, that appeal was set aside in favor of a more pressing matter.

The next month, on Halloween afternoon, Dr. Story was, without warning, arrested on Lovell's Main Street and charged with twelve counts of sexual assault.

CHAPTER 13

"Would you believe that four police cars converged on Dr. Story as he entered a hardware store?" Jan Hillman asks bitterly when she discusses that day when one of Lovell's most respected citizens was arrested on Main Street.

"Of course if all the police department personnel who were related to the accusers had been there," she adds, "there would have been even more!"

This startling statement is backed up by a diagram drawn by the Story family in the early stages of the case. (Illustration)

During the evening hours of October 31, 1984, the doctor's office was searched, his examining table and records confiscated and he was taken to Big Horn county jail in Basin, forty-one miles south of Lovell. On the way, a stop was made at South Big Horn County Hospital, where a blood test was taken to determine whether or not Dr. Story had fathered a child born to Minda Brinkerhoff. This and a subsequent test both produced negative results.

That time, Doc spent less than eight hours in jail. His friends quickly raised bail and he was back in his home before the night was over, but the real trouble was just starting. A week later, thirteen more

WEB OF RELATIONSHIPS

ACCUSERS

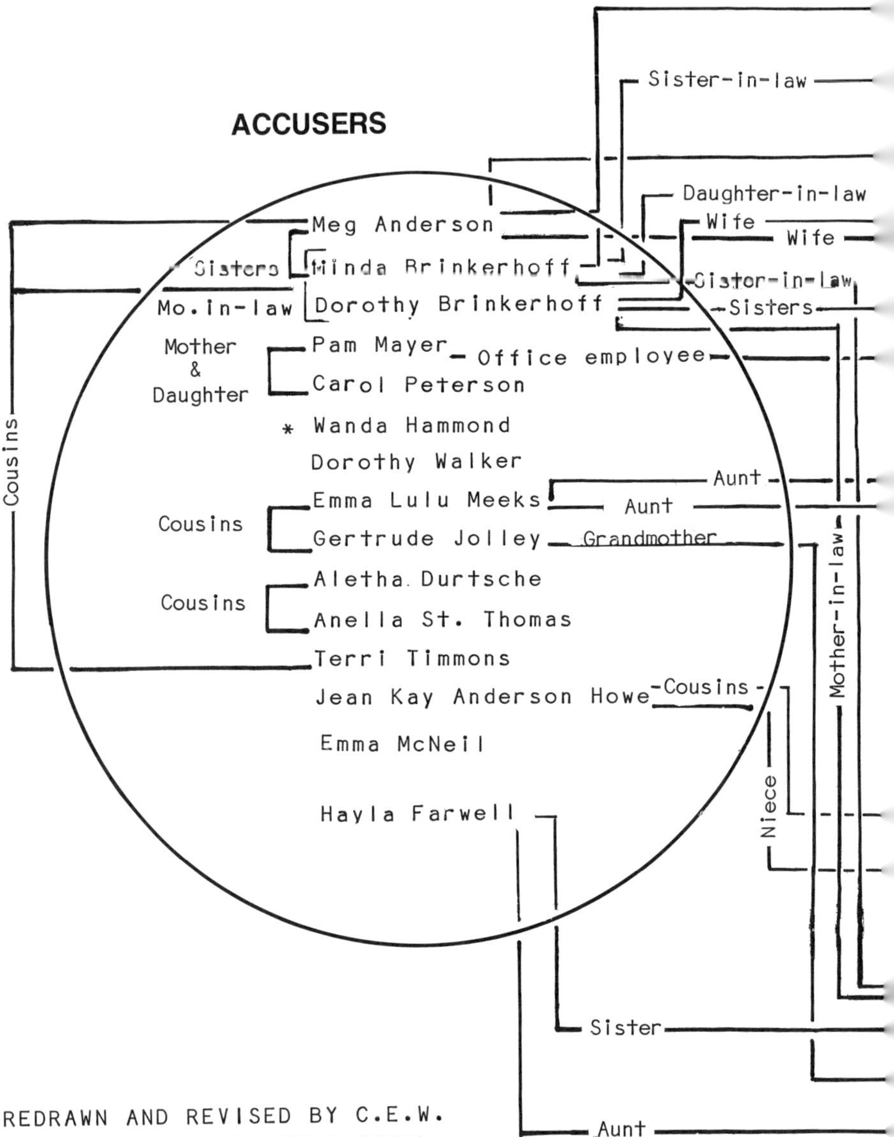

REDRAWN AND REVISED BY C.E.W.
FROM ORIGINAL BY LINDA STORY

* RELATED TO NON-CHARGING ACCUSERS

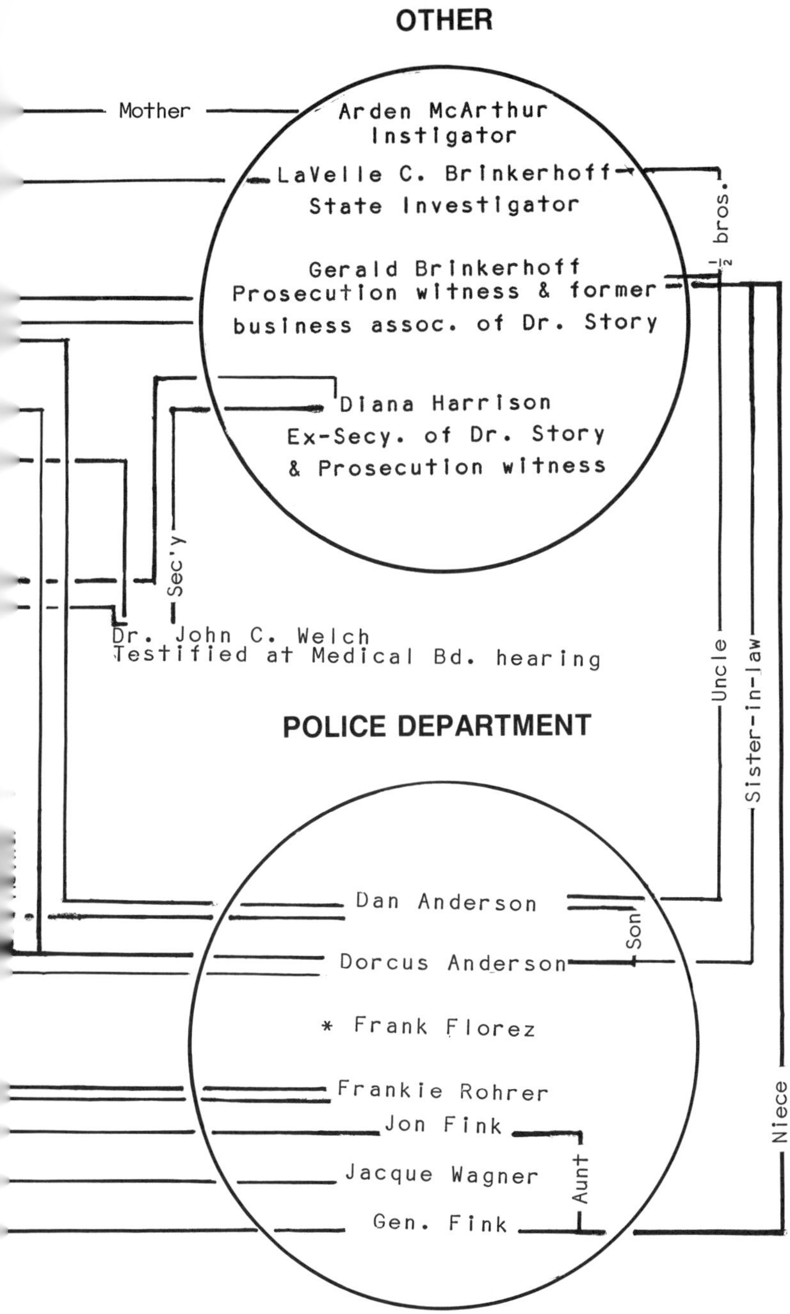

NOTE: Relationships are not fully outlined due to space limitations

charges were added and eight were dismissed by County Attorney Tharp, leaving a total of seventeen charges by nine women. To be very clear here, it must be noted that several of the women were accusing Dr. Story of rape on **more than one occasion!**

Again, as in the cases of Meg and Minda, when several of the women claimed to have been assaulted repeatedly by Dr. Story, the doctor and his family and friends took heart. Surely no one could really believe that even one woman could allow herself to be raped more than once by the same man - by appointment - regardless of background, upbringing or even mentality. That several claimed to have done so, seemed to put the entire episode in the realm of fantasy.

Unfortunately, women on the jury were literally overwhelmed by the weight of numbers, and in spite of Mr. Aarestad's entreaties to "apply the test of reason" to the testimony they had heard, they found Dr. Story guilty in six of the nine cases. Only one of the three thrown out was a complaint of multiple assaults.

"The number of accusers led the court and jury to accept what was said by one witness as being supported by others' testimony, rather than analyzing each case independently," Aarestad said, "In spite of no physical evidence whatsoever, the repetition of testimony snowballed."

Mr. Aarestad made a good point, but to say that was the only reason for Dr. Story's conviction would be over-simplification. From the beginning, doors were closed to Dr. Story and opened for his accusers by law enforcement, investigators and finally the court, by way of the law itself.

Tracing the intricate paths of deception, inconsistencies and outright lies which led to an innocent man's conviction, might never have been accomplished if it were not for that group of people who call themselves simply, "the defense committee," who have literally dedicated their lives to poring over records and following leads.

It is a sad and frustrating and sometimes seemingly hopeless task, but with the tenacity demonstrated by Jan Hillman and Wes Meeker and others undiminished, it too, has snowballed and they are still confident that justice will prevail in the end.

CHAPTER 14

Investigation based on rumors and gossip turned out to be more than Lovell Police Chief David Wilcock could handle.

Described by the media as a "short, heavy man with a soft voice and a gentle manner," Wilcock had not yet, in the summer of 1984, proven himself so lovable in Lovell.

Although originally from the Lovell area, he was new in the position of police chief when the Story investigation began and it didn't take many interviews with reluctant women to convince him that he didn't have the necessary expertise to deal with the situation. Neither, he said, was he the "right sex."

Consequently, after taking a number of statements in the summer of 1984, Chief Wilcock hollered for help. County Attorney Terry Tharp agreed that he needed it.

It's a situation men don't relate to very well," Tharp said, and immediately called in a woman to do the job.

She was Judi Cashel, a sergeant on the Casper, Wyoming police force, specially trained in sexual assault investigation.

Sgt. Cashel entered the investigation Sept. 27, 1984 and, according to Catherine Warren, Casper Star Tribune reporter who covered the entire Story case, she went undercover, up to a point.

"Casper Police Sgt. Judi Cashel, with her red hair and earthy sense of humor, could not go unnoticed in a small town, even if she didn't indulge her penchant for wearing 'Dolly Parton' wigs," an admiring Warren said in a lengthy article following Dr. Story's conviction.

Cashel recalled for reporter Warren that she was the object of "gossip." Lovell citizens, she said, thought she was either running a house of prostitution out of her motel room, or was a new secretary at the police station.

It soon became obvious, though, from the steady stream of women in and out of the station, that there was an investigation going on and it wasn't going to help Dr. Story.

First, however, the prospective victims needed to be contacted, and Lovell police furnished a list of women for Sgt. Cashel to interview. According to Dorothy Brinkerhoff, Minda's mother-in-law, the list originated with Arden McArthur, whom she said, "knew a lot of people."

One of the complaints went back to 1959 and several others to the 1960's and 70's and Cashel admitted that by the time she got to the alleged victims, memories had faded and people had moved and married.

"What we got was, 'My cousin told me that...' and "I heard...'" Cashel recalled.

More rumors?

Even when the women came to the station for questioning, Cashel said, it wasn't easy. "Many had never told their parents or husbands what had happened to them and many of them didn't know the correct sexual terms for what had happened in Story's office."

Not included in Sgt. Cashel's assessment of Dr. Story's accusers was that neither did some of them understand the significance of gynecological procedures, but this was common knowledge among his nurses. "Would you believe," one said, "that a woman would get all shook up by a doctor's suggestion that she use her finger to feel the position of an IUD after insertion?"

With her chores completed and safely back in Casper after the trial, Sgt. Cashel fired a parting shot at Lovell in the interview with Catherine Warren. Many of the women had been "raised to be victims," she said, and if she knew, the sergeant probably didn't care what the reaction was to that statement.

Since the majority of women making complaints were Mormon (only two non-LDS victims' cases were brought to trial) other Mormon women were incensed at Sgt. Cashel's implication.

"Our church doesn't teach us to be stupid!" they said, and their non-LDS neighbors weren't happy about it either.

"What does she think, that because we live in a small town, we can't think for ourselves?"

Oprah Winfrey, many months later, in interviewing some of the women who claimed they had been assaulted by Dr. Story, made a similar error. She repeatedly referred to the accusations as "unbelievable," but then attempted to explain them by reminding her audience that the incidents took place in a small town.

Judi Cashel did not endear herself to

Lovell citizens during her stay there, but not for the reasons she cited in the Casper newspaper article.

Townspeople who dined at the Big Horn Restaurant at the edge of town during that period recall that Sgt. Cashel was usually there in the evening and could be seen and heard discussing the day's activities with members of the police force. Since Dr. Story was supposed to be considered innocent until proven guilty, they were resentful of what they felt was a lack of professionalism.

In the Casper Star-Tribune article, Sgt. Cashel was quoted as saying that she interviewed "more than fifty women who had some complaint of sexual misconduct on Story's part," however her court testimony was simply that she had interviewed forty to forty-five women.

Lovell residents agree with her on that. The part that still causes blood pressure to rise is the way the interviews were conducted.

"Her method was to encourage the women to talk to her," Jan Hillman says, "often giving them the 'I am woman, hear me roar,' lecture." She then wrote their statements in her own words and signed them herself. Those which were not detrimental to Dr. Story were destroyed.

One outspoken woman who had not been a patient of Dr. Story's for many years, said in retrospect, "Dave Wilcock called me at work and asked me to come to the police station for an interview and I told him if it was about Dr. Story that he wasn't my doctor." Despite her refusal to appear, the police chief called again, she said, and she did go for the interview.

The investigator was Sgt. Cashel and the woman continues, "I told her too, that he wasn't my doctor, but she still asked me if I'd had some bad experience with him." The woman repeated that Dr. Story was not her doctor, but Sgt. Cashel persisted, saying she "knew" the woman was a patient of Dr. Story's and Blue Cross records were her source of information.

"She kept on trying to get me to say something had happened to me, even asking me, 'Are you sure?' and I kept telling her he wasn't my doctor."

Finally, in anger and frustration, the woman told the investigator how she felt about the interrogation and left.

"I even told her why I stopped going to Dr. Story years ago, which was because he was too slow," she said, "but that wasn't what she wanted to hear."

Sgt. Cashel reappeared on the scene during Dr. Story's criminal trial in April 1985. Spectators in the courtroom reported that the sergeant, who was seated directly in front of and facing the witness box, seemed to be "coaching" the prosecution witnesses with nods, smiles and frowns throughout their testimony.

Since they felt sure it couldn't have escaped the judge's attention, the observers were forced to speculate among themselves that maybe legally there was nothing wrong with such action, but it certainly didn't look fair.

In pre-trial motions, the Court had ordered that all witnesses be excluded from the courtroom before and after their testimony. This order was also to include an injunction against their communicating with one another after testifying. Sgt. Cashel, however, who was obviously friendly to the prosecution witnesses, was given the duty of escorting them from the holding area to the courtroom, on one occasion taking so long to do so that even the judge became impatient.

To think that the sergeant did not take advantage of the opportunity to relay information about previous testimony to the complainants would be naive, her detractors believe.

"She did everything she could to help them," was the subject most discussed by Dr. Story's supporters at the end of those days' proceedings, and several have since signed affidavits confirming that belief.

Researchers into the Story case feel that because interviewees didn't sign their own statements, the voice of conscience may have been muted in some instances. Indeed, one, after a long, seemingly reluctant interview with Attorney Tharp, said, "I don't hate the man."

Women (other than Judi Cashel) who have themselves been raped and/or worked with rape victims, have consistently said that none of the so-called victims in the Story case were "outraged enough."

Many of the women whose statements were used to bring suit against Dr. Story used terms like "it was **probably** his penis," or admitted that even though they had seen nothing and had no reason to suspect any impropriety, they "believed" he had "dilated" them with his penis.*

Another, after referring to the usual "dilation," said that the object inserted felt "warm and like it belonged there," and she "wondered" if Dr. Story had placed his penis in her vagina.

But in spite of discrepancies and vague recollection of details, the investigation continued and before the end of the year, County Attorney Tharp was using Sgt. Cashel's statements to build a case against a medical doctor the equal of which Wyoming and possibly the entire country, had never seen.

* During the time of the Medical Board hearing, Dr. Story was asked if it was his policy to suggest dilating his women patients frequently, and he replied, somewhat wryly, that he had heard that word (dilate) more times during the last few months than he had ever used it.

CHAPTER 15

Carol Peterson and her companion, also from Lovell, were excited. It was a beautiful fall afternoon, with only a hint of the winter to come in the air, perfect for making the drive from Lovell to Basin, Wyoming, Big Horn county seat. Their destination was the county attorney's office.

It had been a little over two weeks since Dr. Story's Main Street arrest and now it looked like the two women were in direct line to be witnesses in his criminal trial. They had both given statements about their experiences with the doctor to Dave Wilcock and then to Judi Cashel. Today they would tell it all again for the benefit of the man who would be the prosecuting attorney.

Neither woman had ever been involved in a court trial before and at first they had been quite nervous with the interviews and everything, but it seemed to be getting easier as they went along. This was the final step and they hoped Mr. Tharp would be easy to talk to, not like some doctors who didn't always want to listen to everything you had to say.

By 3:50 p.m. on November 16, 1984, the two were seated in Terry Tharp's office and he was doing his best to put them at ease by explaining that the purpose of the interview was to go over the statements they had given Judi Cashel. "Are they substantially correct?" he asked.

"Mine is not," Carol's companion said quickly. This was the part she wanted to get past as soon as possible. "It says here," she went on, "that I **believe** Dr. Story inserted his erect penis into my vaginal canal."

This was exactly what was said about the alleged assault, no more or no less, in Judi Cashel's report of September 29, 1984. Now, less than two months later, the incident had become quite startling.

"Actually," she continued, "I know it happened because the last time I was there when he was doing a pelvic, he said, 'I need to dilate you,' and he said 'would you mind guiding this tube in?' I reached my hand for the end of the table, he put his erect penis in my hand and I pulled my hand back and yelled 'no' and he went ahead and just shoved it inside of me."

She needn't have been afraid attorney Tharp would question her about this new version of the alleged rape, because his only comment was, "all right."

In the course of a criminal investigation, it would seem important that such radical changes in any prospective witness's story be closely questioned, but in this case, it was not, according to the investigative report.

The woman's reference to "yelling" and also to force on the doctor's part, if credible, could have been a bonanza for the prosecution, because all of the other accusers had admitted there was no force, no restraint of any kind used by the doctor during the alleged assaults.

There were some problems, though, with both the outcry and the alleged force. Could a woman "yell" in a building with walls described as so thin that conversations could be heard from room to room, and not attract any attention? And of even more consequence, would any woman actually yell "no" at the outset of an assault and then lie quietly while her doctor raped her?

Apparently, Mr. Tharp felt that neither version would go over well with a jury, because this woman was not used as a complaining witness in the criminal trial.*

The balance of her statement that day concerned reasons for a personal animosity toward the doctor and when the interview ended after fourteen pages of accusations, contradictions and discrepancies, the two women had a question.

"Can he sue us when this is over?" they asked.

*The only reason this case is mentioned is to illustrate the hysteria which seemed to propel some of the women involved once the fire of rumor and gossip had been ignited. In only two months, a vague "belief" that something improper had happened, broke out into a full-fledged account of forcible rape.

CHAPTER 16

Attorney Tharp's emphatic assurance that no one would be sued by Dr. Story spoke well for his self-confidence. He evidently felt that he had the ability to keep any discrepanices from surfacing during the trial.

As the interview with Carol Peterson progressed, there were several obvious contradictions in her account of the day she was allegedly raped by her family doctor, but they didn't seem to be worrisome.

For instance, the following exchange:

Tharp: "You didn't feel comfortable with him?"

Carol: "No, I never did. My mom had always trusted him and he had always been my family doctor, but I didn't."

Later, however:

Carol: "No one likes to tell this sort of details about having a **man that you trusted** put his penis inside of you and acting like he is just top dog of the world and you are just a nothing, anyway."

In court, Carol was more dignified and restrained, but apparently had, in the intervening five months, gained total recall. Now, there were no vague references to being "sure that was probably what he was doing." Now she spoke firmly of having lifted the sheet covering her legs and seeing the doctor's erect penis, immediately following the penetration of her vagina.

Further, her knowledge of obstetric procedures had improved noticeably. During her interview with Tharp in his office, she had said it was when Dr. Story suggested a pelvic to check a negative pregnancy test, that she "knew something was wrong."

In court, when asked if she was concerned "in any way" by the doctor's decision to do a pelvic to determine whether or not she was pregnant, she replied primly, "No, because I knew that sometimes a doctor can do a pelvic examination and just by looking at the cervix, he can tell whether a woman is pregnant or not."

In the front row of spectators, directly facing the witnesses, Sgt. Judi Cashel nodded and smiled approvingly.

By court time, Carol had also significantly revised her answer to the question about why she failed to report the rape to the police as soon as it happened. "I was afraid no one would believe me," she said.

In Tharp's office however, Carol had told him, "Because they would have made fun of me," and added, "They would have said, 'just wishing, dreaming.'"

Again it seemed that Attorney Tharp, rather than delve further into reasons and motives, simply papered them over and used the bits and pieces of information which best suited his purpose.

CHAPTER 17

When Arden McArthur stopped Aletha Durtsche on the main street of Lovell in the summer of 1983, Aletha was feeling kind of blue. Things just weren't going right for her at home or at work and she felt like calling Dr. Story, except that the last time she had seen him, he didn't seem as patient and understanding as usual.

"He just didn't seem like Dr. Story," she said later in court. "He always cared so much. And that day he didn't seem like he really cared that much. He didn't seem to be concerned that I really was sick because always before, maybe there wasn't anything wrong with me, but he always made me feel like there was."

So when Arden pulled over in her car and asked Aletha if she could talk to her, Aletha was glad - it would take her mind off her problems.

And it did that. When Arden asked the now-famous question, "Have you ever had any experience with Dr. Story that would make you think he was sexually assaulting you?" it opened up a whole new period in Aletha's life, one which led eventually to national recognition.

Aletha's background reflects a series of emotional crises. She claimed to have been molested by a relative when she was very young and through the years, sexual experiences seemed to be prevalent in her life. Not a secretive person, she sought comfort from her friends and co-workers and her disclosures became, as one listener said, "soap opera time."

Aletha also found a confidant in Dr. Story, and his confiscated records show that she was a frequent patient in his office. She appreciated his concern for her and sometimes brought along a loaf of bread or a batch of cookies. On one occasion, Aletha, a fair artist, painted a picture for the doctor which was still hanging on the wall of his clinic when she brought charges against him.

Once, in 1981, when things were especially bad at home, Aletha first took a handful of aspirin and then fled to the emergency room of North Big Horn County Hospital. There she asked that Dr. Story be called and it was there that he again counseled her in his characteristic calm, matter-of-fact manner.

Even though Mr. Aarestad, Dr. Story's lawyer, was unable to bring this episode out in court, the jury decided in favor of Dr. Story's innocence in Aletha's case.

Mr. Aarestad: "Let's return to the 1968 and 1971 instances (of suspected rape.) You mentioned to your husband, did you not, that you thought Dr. Story had molested you somehow?"

Aletha: "Yes...(in 1971) I came out of Dr. Story's office, got in the pickup (with Mike, then her boyfriend) and I said 'I think Dr. Story just screwed me.' He said, 'on the bill?' and I said, 'no, literally,' and he said, 'Oh, no way, he wouldn't do that. He is your doctor.' And I said, 'maybe he wouldn't - I don't know. And we never mentioned it again."

Later, under further examination, Aletha enlarged upon this incident, saying that in 1968, she was fifteen years old and had never had intercourse. "I **wondered** if that was what he was doing," she said. But in 1971, at age eighteen, she again **thought** Dr. Story had taken advantage of her and this time she was **more sure** because, "I was pregnant then and we weren't married and I had had sex at that time and knew what it felt like," she explained.

Throughout the course of investigative questioning and her court testimony, Aletha stoutly maintained that she had not talked about her problems with Dr. Story to anyone other than an aunt and her Avon lady. The latter came out in court and if it had not been told under such desperate circumstances, would have brought down the house.

Tharp: "Now when you talked to your Avon lady about this complaint, did you discuss specifics with her?"

Aletha: "No, I just said I ought to bill **him** after all my services...she said 'why,' and I laughed and said 'he got his jollies off of me.'"

The jury no doubt found it implausible that Aletha had continued to go to Dr. Story for twelve years after the 1971 episode and further, that when she finally decided in 1983 that she had definitely been raped, she still took her children to him. Although she said under oath that at the time of the alleged assault she was "afraid he would kill me or something," she readily admitted taking her 11-year-old daughter to him a few months later.

One of the most mysterious aspects of the Story case is that Aletha Durtsche was the only one of the women originally accusing Dr. Story of sexual assault to testify against him in criminal court. This would seem to indicate that her incredible story was the best of those considered by the State Board of Medical Examiners, when they voted to revoke Dr. Story's license to practice medicine.

No one yet has been able to explain why those four doctors, in the face of testimony like Aletha's, found Dr. Story guilty of "unethical and unprofessional conduct likely to deceive, defraud or harm the public."

CHAPTER 18

Emma Lu Meeks is a feisty little woman, 76 years old when she testified under oath that Dr. John Story had sexually assaulted her in 1977. With her grey hair in a page boy bob and her jaw set obstinately, she was the testiest of the witnesses, answering tartly, "I don't know," "I don't recall," or "Nope, don't remember," thirty-five times during her comparatively short testimony.

The day it happened, she told Judi Cashel in early October, she made an appointment to see Dr. Story for just what, she was not sure, but thought it might have been hay fever. After suggesting a pelvic examination and placing her in the correct position, the doctor told her he was going to insert a "tube" in her vagina, which turned out to be "the real thing," she said, adding that she had actually seen his penis. This seemed strange, since she made no reference to lifting the sheet over her knees and when questioned in court about whether or not she was draped for the examination, she couldn't recall.

Again, in the months between that interview and the criminal trial, the witness remembered some things but forgot others. Emma Lu recalled not only the exact reason for her visit to the doctor, but their conversation concerning the ailment. In court, she said clearly that she had gone to the doctor to have him look at a rough place on her skin that she thought might be cancer.

Tharp: "What did he say when you showed him the spot?"

Emma Lu: "He just said it was an aging spot and that he would take it off in the office if I wanted him to."

On Emma Lu's medical record, to which the jury had access, there was no indication of a pelvic examination on October 3, 1977, the day she said she was assaulted. Again, it was a case of believing the doctor's records in some cases and not in others, suggesting that he falsified some charts to hide his activities and left others as a paper trail.

After stating that the doctor had tried to insert his penis into her vagina (like the others, from a standing position at the end of the examining table), without success, Emma Lu made the astonishing disclosure that she got up, dressed, went to the desk and wrote a check for $8.00 to pay for the visit. Then she walked home and didn't tell her husband, a police officer, whom she was afraid would do something violent to the doctor. At least that is what she told Sgt. Cashel. In court, under oath, she said her husband, Ted, was not in good health and she "couldn't do that to him."

With no evidence except a woman's allegation, Dr. Story was convicted of second degree sexual assault in the case of Emma Lu Meeks.

Her next door neighbor, best friend and shirt-tail relative, Gertrude Jolley, however, didn't fare so well at the hands of the jury.

CHAPTER 19

If Emma Lu was the fiestiest witness, Gertrude Jolley was the most vague. Tall and dignified, with snow white hair neatly coiffed, she looked like the typical modern grandmother, but her testimony didn't match her appearance.

Gertrude was also in her 70's when she testified that Dr. Story had assaulted her in 1980, and those who knew her were horrified that she had been drawn into the case at all.

It was well known that her life had not been easy, and losing both her husband and a daughter fairly close together had been particularly hard on her. She was in reasonably good health, though, except for a borderline diabetic condition, which Dr. Story was monitoring carefully, and she tried to take care of herself otherwise, so as not to be a burden on her one remaining offspring, Deanna Wagner.

So when Gertrude missed out on the flu shots being given at the senior citizens' center, she said, she made an appointment with Dr. Story to get one. She also felt that she needed her medication updated.

The date was September 23, 1980, she told the police chief, and according to pre-trial investigative reports, neither he,

Attorney Tharp or Judi Cashel questioned the shaky assumptions offered as evidence of wrongdoing on Dr. Story's part. Gertrude changed her story three times before declaring at the end of the interview with Dave Wilcock, "I didn't realize what had happened until I got home and put two and two together."

In court, Gertrude's recollections seemed to have firmed up and she testified that "I felt him ejaculate, so I realized what he was doing to me." This did not square with earlier statements that she had seen nothing and had no apparent reason for believing that she had been raped, except for a discharge after the examination, which she thought was suspicious.

After the examination, Gertrude said in court, she waited for the nurse to come and give her the flu shot she wanted and even after that, continued to wait until the doctor himself came back with her prescriptions.

Fortunately for Dr. Story, his attorney was able to have Gertrude's pre-trial statement read into the court record. That, along with her extraordinary behavior after the alleged "rape," apparently gave the jury some trouble and he was found innocent of her allegations.

Throughout the lengthy trial, there were instances of levity and the public heard of one of them when state newspapers reported that after the alleged assault by Dr. Story, Gertrude went home and inscribed a big red "R" on her calendar. What did that represent, the prosecutor asked, and she answered, "Rape!"

It was also significant in this case,

that Gertrude claimed to have told her daughter Deanna about the incident, but that both Deanna and her husband continued as patients of Dr. Story's until September 1983 three years later. In court, Deanna testified that yes, her mother had told her she thought she had been raped, but she had not asked for, nor had Gertrude volunteered any specifics. Neither the prosecutor nor the defense seemed to find anything strange about this mother-daughter exchange, although Mr. Aarestad did ask, "Are you and your mother close?" to which Deanna replied, "yes," and was thereupon allowed to step down.

It must have been a moment of terrible distress for Deanna, who had enjoyed a mutually respectful relationship with her physician.

CHAPTER 20

Hayla Farwell felt like a dummy. When she told Judi Cashel her story, it seemed pretty easy, but today, in county attorney Tharp's office, when he read what Judi had written down, it didn't sound right and she got mixed up. She almost wished that she hadn't gotten into this, but Mr. Tharp was nice to her and reminded her that she wasn't the one who would be on trial - Dr. Story was.

Had the jury been able to hear Hayla's conversation with Attorney Tharp on that November day in 1984, and compare it to her court testimony in the spring of 1985, they might have taken an entirely different view of the alleged assault.

Tharp: (in his office, after establishing that the alleged rape took place seventeen years earlier) "You had an appointment once a week for four to five weeks for a stomach problem?"

Hayla: "Yes."

Tharp: "And during each of those appointments, according to your statement, you believe you were sexually assaulted by Dr. Story?"

Hayla: " Yes."

But in court,

Tharp: "Did you have any health problems

which made it necessary for you to go to the doctor on a regular basis?

Hayla: No.

Tharp: Calling your attention to the 24th of July, 1967, did you go to the doctor on that particular day?

Hayla: Yes.

What followed was a somewhat disjointed account of having been assaulted in much the same manner as her predecessors, except for the startling allegation that after penetrating her once, the doctor stepped to the side of the table, exposed himself to her, went back to the end of the table and calmly inserted his penis again.

The balance of the testimony did nothing to clarify matters. Hayla, like some of the others, insisted that she had been raped by the doctor on other occasions, but didn't realize it at the time.

"Had you ever been suspicious of anything he had done before?

Hayla: No.

Tharp: You had had several pelvic examinations just prior to this last exam, had you not?

Hayla: Yes.

Tharp: Were you suspicious in any way about those examinations?

Hayla: Not then.

It is to be remembered that the witness was not a young, impressionable girl at the time of her alleged experiences with Dr. Story. Although she described herself to Tharp as a "dumb kid," she was a married woman with two children at that time. When pressed to explain what she meant by "not then," she said, "I got to thinking about it. It was basically the same way he had done the other pelvics."

Before, during and after the trial, sexually experienced women rolled their eyes heavenward at the claims of these accusers who "thought" or "suspected" that they had been assaulted.

"Either you've been raped, or you haven't been raped," Jan Hillman said for them all on a "60 Minutes" segment nearly a year later.

It would be charitable to leave the witness here, without exposing the rest of her questionable testimony, but it is too important to ignore. In her pre-trial statement, Hayla said she had told no one about the assault until "several years later." In court, she changed that to having told her mother immediately after the incident. Strangely enough, her mother continued to be treated by Dr. Story until 1983, and several times even took Hayla's children to him. Both she and Hayla admitted this in court, but when defense counsel attempted to cross examine Marie Fink, Hayla's mother, on this critical point, an objection by the prosecution was sustained and nothing was accomplished.

Hayla herself, although answering "no" to the question, "Did you continue to treat with the defendant?" admitted returning either to Dr. Story's office or seeing him as a hospital out-patient on four different occasions between the date of the alleged rape in 1967, and February 1978, eleven years later. This, too, failed to impress the jury with the inconsistency of the whole story.

In Tharp's office, on November 12, 1984, Hayla was belligerent. "I told him I'd fight him over his bill if he tried to collect it," she said, but in court, under oath, it came out quite differently.

Tharp: "Did you ever pay the bill?"

Hayla: "Yes."

Tharp" "When?"

Hayla: "It took a couple of years but we paid it."

Tharp: "Do you recall when you paid it off?"

Hayla: "No."

Tharp: "Was it prior to 1978 or after 1978?"

Hayla: "I think it was after 1978." (shortly after the last treatment by Dr. Story and eleven years after the alleged assault).

Tharp: "Had you been threatened with any kind of action on that bill if you didn't pay it"?

Hayla: "Yes, collection."

Tharp: "Why did you go ahead and pay the bill?"

Hayla: "There were other things on that bill that I didn't object to paying."

To the average woman, the whole supposition of sexual assault on the examining table of a trusted physician is so outrageous, so unacceptable, that the thought of paying the bill for that action simply boggles the mind. Yet, the bemused jury apparently accepted this as a normal reaction to the threat of being turned over to a collection agency.

To his credit, defense counsel attempted to impeach Hayla's testimony that she failed to report the incident to the police because she was sure they wouldn't believe her. Mr. Aarestad knew, like everyone else in the courtroom, that Hayla's brother, Jon, was employed by the Lovell police department at the time of the alleged assault, but his efforts to pursue this pertinent fact were stalled by an objection from the prosecuting attorney, sustained by the judge.

In spite of these inconsistencies and Mrs. Farwell's obviously faulty memory about many of the details of the alleged incident, the jury (again with no evidence except the woman's word) found Dr. Story guilty of assault and battery with "intent to rape."

Even this was inconsistent with the testimony, in which Hayla claimed to have been penetrated twice during the same examination.

During its October 1986 term, the Wyoming Supreme Court heard an appeal by Dr. Story's new attorney (retained shortly after the conviction) Gerald R. Mason of Pinedale, Wyoming. As the result, Hayla's was the only case to be overturned by the state's highest court, leaving Dr. Story with now five convictions, rather than six.

CHAPTER 21

In 1976-77, state legislatures were under pressure by women's groups across the country to ratify the Equal Rights Amendment. Feeling the compulsion even more than most were the Wyoming lawmakers, whose state bears the nickname "The Equality State," and whose heroine is Esther Hobart Morris. A statue of this venerated lady stands before the main entrance of the state capitol and feminists gather periodically to lay fresh flowers in her arms. The inscription at her feet reads, "Proponent of the legislative act which in 1869 gave distinction to the Territory of Wyoming as the first government in the world to grant women equal rights."

The Honorable Cal Taggart of Lovell, was personally convinced that the ERA itself was an innocuous document, short and to the point, but had to acknowledge later that some of the proposed bills which accompanied it were not.

Esther Eskens, wife of another Lovell physician, was a member of the Wyoming House of Representatives at that time and was particularly active on the "Rape Committee." It was this body which set about to amend the sexual assault law in Wyoming, even though statistics showed that it was not difficult to get rape convictions in the

Equality State. "Almost three times more convictions are obtained than acquittals or dismissals," it was reported.

Nevertheless, the Rape Committee went full steam ahead with their intent to better the odds and with the encouragement and guidelines provided them by the National Organization of Women (NOW), they came up with a draft which Esther, as subcommittee chairman, circulated among county attorneys for their input. It was to her that the resulting correspondence was addressed and copies were obtained from the public records of the Legislative Service Office in Cheyenne for this account.

From Platte County Attorney Fred W. Phifer on April 9, 1976: "I don't agree with 6-63.11 which makes corroboration (of sexual assault) unnecessary. I don't think there has to be an eye witness, but there must be some physical evidence, either of the victim's physical condition or surrounding circumstances to go along with the victim's testimony, or the opportunities for injustice are too great...The way that 6-63.11 reads now, **a man could be literally convicted on the victim's sworn accusation.** This is wrong, and it is unnecessary intrusion into the judicial process." (emphasis added)

Attorney Phifer could not have predicted the Story case any better had he possessed supernatural powers.

Sweetwater County Attorney Robert Bath also objected in a letter dated May 14, 1976.

"I took one look at the proposed bill for rape and other sexual offenses and shuddered," he wrote.

"Your proposed bill would raise a multitude of constitutional questions," he said, and "...it is greatly ambiguous and opens the door for a multitude of spurious and fallacious charges." He, too, foresaw what happened to Dr. Story as a frightening possibility.

Caught up in the enthusiasm for women's rights and egged on by a strong feminist influence in the state, however, House and Senate members alike swept aside the objections of thoughtful and discerning attorneys and in their 1977 session, passed House Bill No. 61, Sexual Assault Laws Revision, sponsored by the Joint Judiciary Interim Committee.

Two sections in the new law would eventually contribute to the downfall of Dr. John Story.

1. "W.S. 6-63.11. Corroboration of a victim's testimony is not necessary to obtain a conviction for sexual assault," and

2. "W.S. 6-63.12...if evidence of the prior sexual conduct of the victim, reputation evidence or opinion evidence as to the character of the victim is to be offered, the following procedure shall be used:

"A written motion shall be made by the defendant to the court at least ten days prior to the trial stating that the defense has an offer of proof of the relevancy of evidence of the sexual conduct of the victim and its relevancy to the defense;

"The written motion shall be accompanied by an affidavit... in which the offer of proof shall be stated;

"If the court finds the offer of proof sufficient, the court shall order a hearing in chambers and at the hearing allow the questioning of the victim regarding the offer of proof made by the defendant and other pertinent evidence;

"At the conclusion of the hearing, if the court finds that the probative value of the evidence is substantially out-weighed by the probability that its admission will create a substantial danger of undue prejudice, the evidence shall be admissible pursuant to this section. The court may make an order stating what evidence may be introduced by the defendant, which order may include the nature of the questions to be permitted."

Jan Hillman, who is a successful businesswoman in her own right, is a determined advocate of women's rights, but not, as she points out, at the expense of men's rights.

"We on the defense committee are quite aware of the abuse of women at all levels of society," she says, "and of the need to protect legitimate rape victims from further abuse by the law, but an amendment which can so easily convict an innocent man is surely not what the legislature intended."

Her view is belatedly shared by Polly Boggess, also of Lovell, who was one of the governor's appointees to Wyoming's Commission for Women in 1977.

"It was never the intent of the Women's Commission or the legislature to create a climate favorable to false allegations of rape, but that is what happened," she says now with deep regret.

CHAPTER 22

Dr. Henry Eskens, whose politician wife was instrumental in getting the amendment to the sexual assault law passed in Wyoming, left Lovell in the late '70's to practice in Casper, stating at the time that the new location, more centrally located, would be advantageous to both him and Esther, who was by then solidly entrenched as a member of Wyoming's House of Representatives.

Eskens, whose practice in Lovell was reasonably successful, is also short, stockier in build than Dr. Story and has a completely different temperament. Of Dutch origin, he is brusque in speech and retains a heavy accent, appealing to some patients, but deplored by others as a "poor bedside manner." One employee described him as a "perfectionist," from whom she learned a great deal.

After a few years in Casper, the Eskens' moved to Evanston, a boom town on the western edge of Wyoming where energy development was attracting professional people as well as blue collar workers. By so doing, they also increased the distance between themselves and Lovell's problems.

Henry and Dr. Story had never been compatible - their philosophies differed on nearly every point. But in a small town like Lovell, professional men make an effort to present a united front and so their mutual animosity seldom surfaced, except for an occasional sharp word or two exchanged in a hospital corridor.

When Dr. Story was brought to trial for raping his female patients, Dr. Eskens was subpoenaed as a prosecution witness. However, during pre-trial negotiations between Mr. Aarestad, prosecutor Tharp, Michael Blonigen, an assistant in the Attorney General's office on behalf of the State, and Gary Hartman, Judge of the Fifth Judicial District of Wyoming, Mr. Aarestad protested vigorously.

Since Dr. Eskens' statement consisted of an account of several women patients coming to him complaining of sexual misconduct on Dr. Story's part, Aarestad objected on the grounds of hearsay. Blonigen countered with a lengthy argument disputing that the testimony would be hearsay, but would serve as proof that accusations had been made. Aarestad then changed his objection to one of irrelevancy.

"When they (prosecution) say the statement is offered not as hearsay, but simply to prove that a statement was made, then we move into a relevancy objection," Aarestad said, "...his (Dr. Eskens') statement indicates that he does not know who these people were - they were just general statements pertaining to acts of sexual misconduct that allegedly happened to unidentified patients of Dr. Eskens," he said.

"I don't see where that would ever be admitted on any grounds of relevancy whereby they could offer the statement for that purpose simply to prove that it was made."

Gobbledygook on both sides? To the untrained ear, yes, but it apparently made sense to the judge and the three lawyers involved. Hartman ended the matter by saying to Mr. Aarestad, as he had many other times in reference to testimony by the prosecution, "Again, this is another situation the Court is going to have to reserve its ruling on until that evidence is proffered to the Court. I would presume you would make the objection at the appropriate time and the Court would then have to make a ruling on it."

As it turned out, Dr. Eskens was not called to testify at Dr. Story's criminal trial. So why is it mentioned at all? Simply because Henry, apparently not satisfied with his exclusion from the legal proceedings, held a news conference with Catherine Warren of the Casper Star-Tribune in October 1985, four months after Dr. Story's sentencing.

With Dr. Story already convicted, Dr. Eskens' motives are not clear for trying to add to the weight of evidence against his former colleague, but he seemed determined to get into the act.

"Patients were coming into my office and into my living room seven days a week crying and complaining," he said, and "that was the No. 1 reason we left Lovell. I just couldn't stomach that filth."

The Evanston doctor, himself the defendant in two malpractice cases at the time, said in the same interview that he had written to the Board of Medical Examiners about the situation in Lovell, but they did nothing.

"It was as if they were saying, 'Henry, how dare you talk that way about your colleague?'" he said.

His bizarre remarks brought instant response, not only from some of his former employees, but from Dr. Cohen, the Medical Board's executive secretary.

Board officials had said repeatedly that searches of their files had turned up nothing on Dr. Story and now, with this latest intimation of negligence or indifference on their part, Dr. Cohen blew up.

"If a (further) search of the files reveals nothing," he said, "I intend to personally see whether Eskens committed libel in making those statements against the board.

In spite of (or perhaps because of) the friction between himself and Dr. Story, Dr. Cohen was particularly concerned about the appearance of a cover-up by his board.

"We don't lose those types of things," he continued, and "I'm madder than hell about these current allegations."

Dr. James T. Sampson, Cohen's predecessor as board executive, held the position during the years Eskens claimed to have written letters of complaint about Dr. Story. He too, reacted indignantly.

"I can't imagine the board ignoring something like that," he said, "I have no recollection of it whatsoever."

According to the October 10, 1985 edition of the Casper Star Tribune, board officials stated that every complaint filed against a physician is kept on file permanently, but said they found no complaints prior to the 1980's against Dr. Story.

One of the plaintiffs in the Story trial, Annella St. Thomas, and her husband, Nelson, also claimed to have written the board and received a reply from them, the details of which they could not recall. Moreover, the letter was destroyed, they said, so there was no proof of its existence.

Dr. Cohen explained this by saying he believed that the couple might have "honestly believed" they were corresponding with the medical board, but were instead dealing with the Wyoming State Medical Society, a private group. The president of that group also said at the time of the trial that he knew of no such complaints and found it very unlikely that his society would have lost or destroyed such a "sensitive" document.

From the other end of the spectrum came rebuttals from former employees of Dr. Eskens.

In a letter to the Lovell Chronicle and the Casper Star-Tribune, Louise Zeller, who had worked for him for five years, gently refuted Henry's contention.

"Part of my responsibility was recording the patient's reason for consultation (with Dr. Eskens) and never once did I write down a complaint of sexual harrassment by Dr. Story, or hear Dr. Eskens mention anything on that subject, though **"he was very open about everything else."** (emphasis added)

Louise, a deeply spiritual young woman, had reason to admire Dr. Story and his family and to be profoundly distressed by the allegations against him. During the last few years of his life, her Methodist minister grandfather had made his home with her, and her loving care and attention to his welfare were well known in Lovell. Dr. Story had attended to his physical needs with the respect due a preacher of the gospel and when the old gentleman's eyesight failed, Marilyn Story volunteered time each week to visit with him and read his mail or whatever other material had accumulated.

Louise continued in her letter, "Before going to work for Dr. Eskens, I worked at the hospital and nursing home for eight years and would hear the normal talk at the nurses' station between physicians and RN's. Never once did I hear Dr. Story make back-alley comments. Neither did I ever hear anything said about him except the highest praise for his competence and professionalism."

Another former employee of Dr. Eskens', Barb Shumway, brought another inconsistency to light.

"When Dr. Eskens left Lovell," she said, "he called all of us (employees) in and recommended that we go to Dr. Story after he left. Most of us did and had a good relationship with him."

The Story case needed no further intrigue, but the Eskens "exposé" was just another twist in an ever-growing maze of misinformation.

CHAPTER 23

Terri Hansen Timmons and her allegations against Dr. Story were somewhat different from any of the other witnesses at his criminal trial.

Born in Lovell in 1952, she was the youngest of the accusers and by most standards, the best looking. Slim, with long dark hair worn slightly curled at the ends and straight, eyebrow-hiding bangs, she gave the impression of a fairly self-confident young woman, except for some involuntary facial distortions during her testimony. Her demeanor was modest, her voice well modulated and she spoke easily as the prosecutor drew her gently into an account of statutory rape.

Her experience, she said, went back sixteen years to an examination performed when she was a teenager. Although the doctor's records showed no pelvic given her on that day, and that the reason for her visit was a cold, she denied all that and said she had gone for a chronic menstrual problem, for which Dr. Story had given her a pelvic examination three months earlier.

It is probably to be expected that expressions like "totally nude" sound more ominous when applied to a teenager than to a mature woman in such a situation, and

Attorney Tharp played on this to win the sympathy of the jury for an innocent child. Mrs. Timmons, crying at times, testified to feeling something "very, very warm and soft" next to her vagina and then to having this object "pushing inside of me."

It hurt, she said, but the doctor continued to push until "he pulled it out all of a sudden and I felt the warm fluid go down my bottom."

On the face of it, and considering the emotional impact on the jury, this was probably the most convincing of the nine accusations heard during the trial, but on close examination, it too, was neither consistent nor believable.

Although Mrs. Timmons, under oath, said that she recognized the object placed in her vagina as "bare flesh," she further testifed that in telling her grandmother about it immediately following the incident, she said only that "he hurt me." Considering the fact that she described everything else about the examination as "hurting her," this hardly seemed proof of rape. To observers, it seemed that here was a logical place for some vigorous cross examination, but it never came. Instead, defense counsel pursued a line of questioning about the location of the examining room, the exact position of the cloth drape across the patient's knees and other maddeningly minor details until the audience was fidgeting and the jury dozing.

Further, Terri testified that while she had "never seen a nude man," she "suspected" it was the doctor's penis that entered her vagina. Surely to a virginal youngster, rape would be so painful and frightening that she could not suppress an outcry of some kind, but she testified only to crying and lying quietly until the doctor left the room and then returned to tell her to get dressed.

Although she said she had never told her parents, she did tell her sister several days after the incident. It was not until her marriage seven years later, however, that she realized what had happened to her.* This was not pursued in court by defense counsel, but in his closing arguments, Mr. Aarestad asked the jury to consider how Terri could have told her sister something that she herself didn't figure out for seven years. It was a good observation, but came too late to be effective.

After Terri was married, it took another eight years (and some prodding by the McArthurs in 1984) to accuse Dr. Story of rape.

Questioned by the prosecutor as to why she had kept the secret, Terri answered vaguely, "because of how things were in our family." This was not followed up by either prosecution or defense, and supposedly explained why Terri's parents continued to make appointments for her with Dr. Story during the remaining four years that they lived in Lovell, and she kept them, even undergoing at least one other pelvic examination from him without incident, she said.

Again, without evidence, only a woman's allegation, Dr. Story was found guilty of first degree rape in Terri's case.**

* This was reminiscent of the claims of another woman, who said in the earliest stages of the investigation, that as a 33-year-old virgin, she went to Dr. Story for a pre-marital examination. It was uncomfortable, but it was not until her wedding night several weeks later that she knew her physician had had intercourse with her. "It was the same pinching, hurting feeling," she told her husband, and then "forgot about it" until 1983, when she was contacted for a statement.

**Terri Timmons was another of the women who appeared on the Oprah Winfrey Show in 1986. Although her husband, Lloyd, had not been called to testify in court, he was questioned by their hostess at the conclusion of the program and his declaration that he was proud of Terri and the other ladies for coming forward with their stories was admiringly received. The notable exception in the audience was Dr. Story's sister, Gretchen, who bravely defended her brother in the face of overwhelming prejudice against him, and whose efforts were ridiculed and cut short by the bouncy Oprah.

CHAPTER 24

Wanda Hammond, short, dark, stocky and easily moved to tears, shared a school bus route with her husband. On October 4, 1968, fifteen years before accusing Dr. John Story of raping her, she had the last school district-ordered physical examination from Dr. Story that she was ever to have. It was not her last visit, however - on December 13, 1968, the date that she picked from Dr. Story's confiscated office records, she went to him for an entirely different reason from that which she stated in her sworn testimony.

Wanda's first contact with law enforcement personnel was her interview with Judi Cashel on October 4, 1984 and went like this:

"This incident involved Ms. Hammond being sexually assaulted by Dr. J. H. Story at his office...Ms. Hammond recalls that it was in the fall of the year, as she was employed as a school bus driver. Mrs. Hammond had a 2:00 p.m. appointment which she believes was because of a cold she was suffering from. Ms. Hammond recalls that she had to wait until the office was nearly empty before she saw the doctor. She did not get out of the office until approximately 5:30 p.m. which caused her husband to have to leave his work early to drive the school bus in her place.

"Ms. Hammond said that Dr. Story told her that she needed a pelvic examination. Ms. Hammond said that she did not understand why she needed a pelvic examination as it had nothing to do with her complaint. However, Ms. Hammond did not question the doctor about his decision. Ms. Hammond recalls that Dr. Story began the examination by checking with one and then two fingers. At that time, Dr. Story told Ms. Hammond that he was now going to use another type of instrument, which was a little larger. Dr. Story then attempted to insert what Ms. Hammond recognized to be his penis. Dr. Story asked Ms. Hammond if she would like to guide it in. Ms. Hammond replied negatively. However, Dr. Story reached for her hand and placed it in the area of Ms. Hammond's vaginal opening. Ms. Hammond stated that at that time, 'I felt his hair and I felt him.' Ms. Hammond said that she said 'what are you doing?' and began to squirm. Dr. Story turned away at that time."

This account seems clear enough and may even contain a grain of truth, but when compared with other statements and examined in the light of hard evidence, it is weak indeed.

On November 12, 1984, Wanda was summoned to the office of County Attorney Tharp, where she told the story over again, but with some significant changes.

First, the date of the offense now became, not a vague "in the fall," but a definite "October 4, 1968," the result of having been allowed to peruse her own billing records and make the determination as to the exact day. After the incident, she said, Dr. Story turned his back on her and she "heard him zip his pants up."

The most interesting portion of this investigative interview, however, lies in the last question and answer.

Tharp: "Have you ever been back there since?"

Wanda: "Not that I recall, because I can remember telling myself that this would be the last time I would ever go to him. I changed doctors."

While on the mild side for the reaction of a rape victim, this made more sense than the reality.

What really happened was that on October 4, 1968, Wanda's appointment was for a bus driver's examination and on December 13, 1968, she did return to Dr. Story. Moreover, by the time her case was presented to the jury, the date of the assault had been changed to December 13, 1968, thereby eliminating the need to explain why she would return to the doctor whom she said had sexually assaulted her two months previously.

There was a problem, though, when Wanda was allowed to change the date, because her medical record showed that on December 13, 1968, Wanda Hammond's appointment with Dr. Story was not for the relief of cold symptoms, as she had consistently stated, but **to have an intrauterine, or birth control, device inserted!**

The jury, however, heard about that only through the context of Dr. Story's denial under oath that he had ever assaulted the 55-year-old witness. Reading from her medical chart concerning the December 13 visit, he said not only that Wanda had requested and he had placed the IUD in her uterus, but that it was one of the sterile procedures which required the presence of a nurse in the office.

Aarestad: "When you have a sterile procedure such as implantation of an IUD, does that result in a nurse being present?"

Doc: "The nurse has charge of the whole sterile setup. It does require her being present".

Aarestad: "So on that day, December 13th, the nurse would have been present?"

Doc: "She would have had to have been on that particular day."

This procedure would also explain Wanda's recollection that the doctor had placed her hand in the area of her own vagina, since it is common practice for a physician to instruct his patient in the correct placement and how to determine it. That Dr. Story's attorney, Wayne Aarestad, failed to subpoena the nurse who was indeed present during the incident, is another question not fully answered, but Marilyn Story believes that because the nurse involved suffered from a recurring illness for many years, she was too ill at that time to testify at the trial. Never fully recovering, she died in 1986, but the fact that Dr. Story had indeed fitted Wanda Hammond with an IUD during that last appointment has since been established by other means.

Dr. Story's testimony in his own behalf was the first and only reference in court to Wanda Hammond's obvious "mistake," and Prosecuting Attorney Tharp wasted no time in arranging for Wanda to reappear as a "rebuttal witness" after the defense had concluded its case. At that time, he asked her the question, "...did he (Dr. Story) ever insert an IUD in you?" to which Wanda replied that she was "positive" he had not.

Consistent with that testimony, Wanda, during the trial and throughout the following months, repeated over and over that what made the apointment memorable was that Dr. Story insisted on doing a pelvic examination, when her only complaints were cold-related. Completely ignored was the evidence on her chart which, in the nurse's handwriting, stated clearly, "wants IUD," and the doctor's own notation that he had placed one for her.

This blatant disregard for the facts and for ordinary office procedure caused Dr. Story's nurses a great deal of frustration.

"What do they think? That we would falsify records for our boss, so that he could rape his women patients?" Nita Bronkema and Judy Gifford, both highly qualified registered nurses, completely dedicated to their profession, found it hard to believe that investigators would so discredit their integrity. But it happened, and now the undoing of the wrong has been found to be much more difficult than instigating the original investigation.

There are several other interesting facets to the Wanda Hammond accusations. Although she stated under oath that she had told her mother about the alleged assault by Dr. Story "approximately nine months after it happened," her mother, LuNita Thompson, who had been the Story children's favorite baby-sitter, continued to be treated by Dr. Story until January 8, 1980, **12 years later**, and also carried on the same warm and affectionate friendship with the whole family.

Parthena Thompson, Wanda's sister-in-law, even now is a strong supporter of Dr. Story and throughout the months since his conviction has said repeatedly that Wanda perjured herself when she denied ever having been fitted for an IUD by the doctor. Parthena allowed this information to be used in a motion seeking a new trial for the imprisoned physician in June of 1987, but in August, the motion was denied on a technicality.

Another interesting sidelight on the Wanda Hammond matter is the way a third person, known to be unfriendly to the doctor, tried to strengthen Wanda's case.

In an interview with Judi Cashel, Ina Welling, a former receptionist for Dr. Story, stated that at some time during her employ, Wanda Hammond had come to the office for a pelvic examination by Dr. Story, and on preparation for it, had become "almost hysterical, begging (me) to stay with her."

Strangely, Mrs. Welling's statement was not used as court testimony and when asked about prior examinations by Dr. Story, Wanda Hammond said clearly that until her last appointment, she had never had reason to question his behavior toward her.

"And did you trust him?" she was asked by the prosecution, to which she replied, "yes."

Even stranger, Wanda identified Ina Welling as the person at the desk when she arrived for her appointment on the day she said she was assaulted, but could not remember if Ina was the one who prepared her for the examination and certainly gave no indication that she had asked her to stay in the room with her on that day or any other.

Ina Welling was discharged from the doctor's employ and one patient says in retrospect, "I don't know how he put up with her as long as he did. One day when I was there, she had patterns and materials for her daughter's wedding at the office and spent the whole time I was there discussing the wedding plans with friends and acquaintances who happened to be in the waiting room. I had a very sick little girl with me and I was offended by the non-stop dialogue, which had no place in a doctor's office."

Throughout the investigation and actual trial of Dr. John Story, inconsistencies and discrepancies, if not outright lies, plagued the prosecution, but they were time after time successfully buried or dismissed as irrelevant. On the other hand, half-hearted attempts by defense counsel to bring them out into the open were completely ineffective.

CHAPTER 25

Annella St. Thomas, too, is dark and heavily built. Her florid complexion and overbright eyes give her a feverish look which belied her calm demeanor on the stand. She was thirty-six years old at the time she testified against Dr. Story, saying he had assaulted her on his examining table eleven years before.

Annella's story was almost identical to those which had been told before, except for one striking detail. She had not only been raped while undergoing a pelvic examination, she said, but immediately following that incident, the doctor had stepped to the side of the table to perform a breast examination and she felt something "poking her in her right side," looked down and saw his "fully erect penis."

What the doctor planned to do next was never learned, as Annella said it was at that point that a nurse knocked on the door and called Dr. Story to the telephone. Neither do court records explain how the doctor escaped notice when he left the examining room in that condition. Wayne Aarestad, defense counsel, mentioned this in his closing arguments.

" ...then it is unclear whether Dr. Story just walks to the door with his organs still exposed or whether he goes to a towel rack somewhere and grabs a towel and holds it in front of him or tucks it in his pants or whatever."

By the time he returned to the examining room, Annella said, she had "regained her composure," was dressed and ready to leave the office.

The "poking" allegation was only too familiar to Dr. Story and his supporters. Although the jury had never heard it, Minda McArthur Brinkerhoff, one of the original accusers, had said exactly the same thing. It was thought at the time to have been one of the reasons Minda's case was not considered credible enough for inclusion in the criminal trial. Indeed, a clinical psychologist diagnosed her description of a penis touching her hip and hand as the result of "hallucinations and illusions being the cumulation of expanding neurotic-psychotic invoking experiences over the years."

Dr. Wrung, well-acquainted with both accused and accusers, observed that a penis which could reach from the edge of the examining table to the patient's body and "poke" her, would have to be "minimally ten inches long." His court testimony included the comment that "I frankly don't know of any human being with a penis that long." Even this graphic comment didn't take into consideration the angle of the male penis at erection - hardly a position to "lie across the table" and "poke" the victim, as both Annella and Minda claimed.

Again, the defense sought to impeach the witness' credibility by inferring that her memory was bad. Questions as to placement of the table in the room, whether it was right or left breast being examined, where the instruments used in the examination were located in relation to the table, what the doctor was wearing, all failed to accomplish the purpose and the jury returned a verdict of guilty of assault and battery with intent to commit rape, again without evidence other than a woman's assertion.

Also interesting is that both Mrs. St. Thomas and her husband, Nelson, testified that they had reported the alleged sexual assault to the Lovell police several weeks after it supposedly occurred. Their first contact was with then Chief Lamar Averett, who said on the stand that he "didn't believe them, because there was no evidence," and later to officer Norm Doerr, who by the time of the trial had been dead for several years.

The St. Thomases also stated that Annella had written a letter to the State Board of Medical Examiners and received a reply saying the board already had one complaint against Dr. Story. This should have come as a great surprise to Mr. Tharp, who had surely read Nelson St. Thomas's pre-trial statement taken by Judi Cashel, in which he said the letter from the Board stated "they would need more corroborative evidence before they could proceed."

Unfortunately, the jury didn't hear the first version and although Mr. Aarestad quickly moved to strike the second one about the board having received a prior complaint, from the record, the damage was done. The jury, although admonished by the judge to forget they had heard it, were no doubt impressed by what seemed to be probative evidence.

Throughout the proceedings, from medical board hearing to conviction in criminal court, no complaints against Dr. Story made prior to those of the McArthurs, were ever found in the files of any official medical organization. This subject eventually became the source of considerable consternation on the part of the participating doctors, who resented being even indirectly accused of ignoring anything so serious as physician-patient abuse.

Neither were the St. Thomases able to produce the letter they said they received from the Board of Medical Examiners.

Again, the prosecution appeared to have the advantage, when witnesses were allowed to testify to circumstances entirely different from what they had said in investigative reports and the defense failed to follow through on obvious irregularities.

CHAPTER 26

Dr. Rand Flory, who practices medicine in Cody, Wyoming, some forty miles west of Lovell, is small, slightly built and boyish looking. On the last day that he testified for the prosecution in the Dr. Story rape trial, he was smiling a little as he left the courtroom and headed for his car. While he was on the stand today, Mr. Tharp had asked him questions that he felt he answered well and after the last one, he had heard the gasps and titters from the audience when he told about taking his wife to his examining room to do "the experiment."

Earlier, Flory had testified at some length about gynecological procedures, for even though he was not a member of that particular board, he had chosen obstetrics and gynecology as his primary field. He had, at attorney Tharp's suggestion, showed, by means of a skeleton, the "lithotomy" position a woman assumes when undergoing a pelvic examination, and explained some of the technicalities of such treatment. He had also gone over the individual records of the complainants and offered his opinion as to whether pelvics were necessary in each case. The fact that he was unable to read some of Dr. Story's writing and had no personal acquaintance with any of the cases, didn't seem to bother him or the prosecuting attorney. Then today, he had been recalled for a short, but successful performance as a rebuttal witness.

"You have stated that you believe it would be possible to complete an act of sexual intercourse with a woman in the lithotomy position," Tharp said, "and do you still hold that opinion?"

"It is more than an opinion," Rand said with a quick look around the courtroom. "When all this was going on I had always assumed it would be possible and so my wife and I went up to the office and tried it. It is rather clumsy...but it is a possible thing."

Over the embarrassed laughter and whispered comments from the audience, Mr. Aarestad objected to this testimony and asked that it be stricken from the record.

"What the witness did with his wife has absolutely no bearing on this case," he said, but the objection was overruled and the answer stood.

A few seconds later the doctor was allowed to step down and the judge released him to go back to Cody, where he had appointments set up for the afternoon.

The last thing he anticipated was to have two furious women accost him in the parking lot.

The first to reach him was Kay Holm of Lovell, a tall, attractive blonde with fire in her eye.

"How could you do what you just did," she said angrily, "How could you testify against a fine doctor and make him look like a rapist?"

Rand was taken aback. "I only did what

I had to do. I didn't have a choice - I was subpoenaed."

"That's not true," Kay went on, not at all mollified by the doctor's shrug and soft murmur, "I'm sorry." He did that a lot, she said later in a statement to Gerald Mason, Dr. Story's third attorney who took over after the criminal trial.

"You didn't have to imply that there was something wrong with Dr. Story's records. You made statements all through your testimony to make him look like a criminal. Did you know they tried to get a doctor from all over and you were the only one who would testify?"

That shocked Rand. "No, I didn't know that, and I thought I didn't have a choice." He shrugged again and said "I'm sorry," but Kay was far from through with him.

To make matters worse for the beleaguered doctor, a second woman, just as indignant, joined them.

Kay went on. "You may have helped to put an innocent doctor in jail, and ---,"

This seemed to startle the young doctor into a realization he had not had before.

"I don't think Dr. Story is guilty," he said, "In looking over his records, I think he's probably a good and thorough doctor."

This infuriated Kay even more. "How can you say that when you just testified against him? You also implied that it was abnormal to give more than two pelvic exams during a pregnancy. I've had four babies, and I've never had just two pelvics."

She paused, and while Flory was shrugging again, the second woman, Georgette Lewis, landed on him with another question.

"Why on earth would you say that there

should be no discharge after a pelvic exam? I've had four kids, three different doctors and numerous pelvic exams and I've always had a very noticeable discharge!"

Now completely overwhelmed by these angry women and their penetrating questions, Dr. Flory stammered, "Well, I've never asked women if they had a discharge or followed up, so I really don't know."

It was the wrong answer. Georgette lashed out again. "Then why did you say it and imply guilt if you didn't feel he was guilty?"

Then to the two women, who more than anything wanted the best defense possible for their friend and physician, came the most frustrating answer of all.

Backing away from them, face flushed and voice unsteady, Dr. Rand Flory, no longer the self-confident witness, said,"I'm sorry, **they could have cross-examined me.**"

He scurried for his car, and Kay and Georgette looked at one another in despair. They wanted to believe that the women on the jury would come to the same conclusions that they had about the Cody doctor's testimony, but fear suddenly gripped them that common sense might not be enough. Dr. Story's lawyers had consistently contended that reason would prevail and had refrained from using strong tactics in cross examination. Their position had seemed reasonable until now, when the two women were suddenly siezed by the thought, "Why **didn't** they cross examine him?"

Slowly, with heavy hearts, they returned to the courtroom, where the proceedings were concluding and Dr. Story's fate would soon be in the hands of the jury.

CHAPTER 27

On a scale of zero to ten, the credibility of the witnesses against Dr. Story in his criminal trial generally came down between one and two, according to observers who sat through the entire proceedings.

In the case of Emma Briseno McNeil, however, it fell to below zero, which chilled the jury into returning a "not guilty" verdict in her case.

To the women in the courtroom who had rallied around their physician and friend, Emma McNeil's story seemed very little sillier than the other eight, but at least one assertion she made exceeded the norm.

In 1977, Emma took her little girl, two years old, into the examining room with her, she said, which in itself, seemed a bit unusual. Everyone knew that although she had been away for two years, her home was in Lovell and had been since childhood. Surely there was someone who would have baby-sat for her for a few hours. Nevertheless, Emma related under oath that after he placed her in the examining position, Dr. Story asked her if she knew she was pregnant and she answered that she wasn't sure.

Emma: "And he says, 'well, I have this soft, sponge thing I am going to insert in you,' and then my little girl started playing with the lever on the bottom (of the table) and it would go up and down."

Prosecuting Attorney Tharp apparently didn't want the narrative to get side-tracked into something other than rape, so he quickly changed the subject to the witness's recollection of whether or not she had seen a speculum in the room on that day. She said that she had not and he led her easily back into the important part.

"Now, then, you said that the doctor stated he was going to put a soft rubber thing in you?"

"He says it would be like a soft sponge."

"Where was he at the time he said this?"

"Standing at the foot of the table."

"Between your legs?"

"Yes, he was."

So far, so good, but the following statement caused audience and jury alike to exchange astonished looks.

Emma: "Well, like I said, that's when he inserted the soft sponge thing and that's when my little girl started to play with that lever...He got mad about that and said I should have left her home. And then he backed up and that's when I felt the penis come out, it was hard."

Tharp: "You say he got mad and he backed away from you?"

Emma: "Yes."

Tharp: "And what did you feel at that time?"

Emma: "Well, when the penis gets hard when it comes out, that's what I felt."

Emma, in her high school years, had been a friend of Susan Story's. After her marriage to Kenneth McNeil, the couple continued to live in Lovell until 1983, when they moved to Maine. Far from Wyoming, Emma was no doubt a little homesick at times, and her husband's wages as an unskilled laborer probably didn't allow for many trips from Maine to Lovell. The opportunity to fly home and visit her family at the state's expense in exchange for a few minutes in the witness chair, must have seemed appealing. This was not mentioned in cross examination and Mr. Aarestad may have regretted the oversight when one of his chief expert witnesses, a gynecologist from California, was indirectly accused by the prosecution of testifying simply because he was paid a consultant's fee to do so.

Emma's testimony was fairly short and she concluded it with the astounding statement that when she realized what had happened to her, she was "kind of surprised," and on leaving the room, she "went out to the front and got the bill and paid it."

Although the McNeils had been involved in a fee dispute with Dr. Story, Mr. Aarestad was prohibited from bringing this to the attention of the jury, but in the end it didn't matter. Emma had self-destructed.

The only other interesting facet of Emma Briseno McNeil's case was found in an investigative report filed by Lovell Police Chief Dave Wilcock on July 7, 1984. While interviewing Meg McArthur Anderson, the chief asked about a "list" of possible witnesses against Dr. Story.

(There are) "names of Mexicans," he said, to which Minda replied, "yes, just so that it would get it out of the circle that people claim it is only in (Mormon). I think Emma Briseno would come forward and that would pull it away from - because too many people think it is all LDS people and it is not."

Minda continued along this line. "There's a Lutheran lady who is afraid to come forward because she is afraid her husband will kill him."

This lady turned out to be Hayla Farwell, who did indeed testify, but whose husband showed no particular animosity toward the doctor, in fact testifying that he had taken Hayla back to Dr. Story several years after the alleged assault.

These two, Emma and Hayla, were the only non-LDS women to publicly accuse Dr. Story of sexual misconduct, a fact which was carefully noted by his supporters.

In spite of what has been repeatedly reported in the news media, Jan Hillman says at every opportunity, "We have never thought or said that the case against Dr. Story was a conspiracy by the Mormon church. It is much more complex than that, but what we can't help but suspect is that one woman used her **influence in the Mormon church** to incite the original complaints against him."

According to another prominent citizen of the Big Horn Basin, it all happened at a time when the state had need of a "sacrificial lamb," or physician conviction, to help prevent the growing incidence of doctor-patient abuse.

If true, another element was added. Was Dr. Story in the wrong place at the wrong time?

CHAPTER 28

Diana Harrison, long-time secretary-receptionist for Dr. Story, didn't claim to be a victim of her employer.

Rather, as she told Police Chief Dave Wilcock in a lengthy interview, she "used" Dr. Story, by continuing to work for him after she "knew" he was raping his female patients.

Diana, a small, attractive woman in her mid-40's, is married with three children, and had worked for Dr. Story off and on since 1969. Throughout that period she had enjoyed a close relationship with the entire Story family and when the doctor was first accused of sexual misconduct with his patients, Diana was as shocked and horrified as any of his friends. Or so she said. She also claimed to remember the day Minda McArthur had been in the office and, as she put it, "the lying began."

Several women, including Kay Meeker, a Powell, Wyoming resident who even after moving twenty miles away from Lovell, continued to treat with Dr. Story and is one of his strongest supporters, recall clearly their conversations with Diana shortly after the accusations began.

"We sat in her car on Main Street," Kay says, "and I remember her pounding the steering wheel with her fist and declaring that Doc was innocent and it was all lies." To another, Diana vowed she "would do anything to help him."

What happened between May 1983 and April 1985, when she appeared in criminal court as a key witness for the prosecution is another question which may never be answered, but of all the accusers, Diana Harrison is held in the most contempt by Dr. Story's family and friends.

Her knowledge of Dr. Story's improper conduct in his examining room, Diana said to Wilcock in July 1984, began in early 1982. In direct opposition to what she had said prior to the Medical Board hearing, she told him that Emma Lu Meeks, her husband's aunt, came to her specifically to reveal what Dr. Story had done to her and advise Diana to stop working for him before she, too, was raped.

"I believed her, I really did," Diana said, "she is not a liar, she is a good person," and if her declaration several months earlier that the accusations were all "hearsay, nothing but hearsay," were not a matter of record, this would go down as a genuine expression of devotion and faith in a close relative.

Diana's statement continued, "Anyway, at the time, my little girl was born with a birth defect, and I had insurance through Dr. Story, the Medical Association. Well, she had to have surgery. It was a pre-existing condition, so naturally no one else would take us. So in a way I feel bad, I used him, really, I had to have that insurance - my little girl had to have that surgery, which was around $10,000, so I continued to work."

The jury never had a chance to decide if this was a plausible reason for continuing to work for a doctor whom you believed was raping his patients, because they never heard it.

Diana's statement to Chief Wilcock was long and emotional, and in the course of it she made a complete about-face on her reaction to Arden McArthur's original accusations.

In November 1983, Diana had referred to Arden as a "crazy lady," Arden's daughter Minda as "kind of stupid," and Minda's last visit to Dr. Story's office as "when the lying began."

But now, in 1984, Diana hardly mentioned Arden or her daughters and concentrated on the women who had supposedly come to her personally with their complaints against their physician.

Before the interview was over, Diana had disclosed to Dave Wilcock the startling information which was to electrify the jury nine months later and earn her the nickname of "the sniffer."

CHAPTER 29

It was April 9, 1985 at 2:45 p.m. when Diana Harrison took the stand to testify against Dr. John Story, her former employer, personal physician and friend.

It was an unusually warm day for April in the Big Horn Basin and the courtroom was sultry. The jury was no doubt tired, after hearing the testimony of the last three complaining witnesses plus eight others for the prosecution. If their attention was beginning to falter, it was quickly brought up by the sight of Diana Harrison, smartly dressed, skillfully made up and seemingly sincere in her desire to help bring this whole distasteful matter to a conclusion. In a way, Diana would serve to bring some normality into the proceedings which had been lacking so far. One problem, undoubtedly, was the generally plain, if not frumpy, appearance of the "victims."

To the men jurors, particularly, it must have seemed incomprehensible that another man would be so attracted physically by any one of them that he would risk his reputation as a doctor to approach them sexually. Further, their stories, while much the same, suggesting a "modus operandi," were difficult to believe, especially those who admitted continuing to treat with Dr.

Story after their alleged rapes, and/or taking their children to him.

Diana's testimony apparently provided some badly needed reinforcement to the claims made by the nine women who said that, months or years earlier, they had been sexually abused by their family doctor.

Dr. Story's attorney, Mr. Aarestad, had previous knowledge of the testimony Diana Harrison was about to offer, and as soon as Prosecuting Attorney Tharp asked her if she ever had occasion to clean up an examining room, Aarestad called for a bench conference.

There he tried unsuccessfully to sidetrack the coming disclosure. His arguments were strong:

"It is so remote and irrelevant and prejudicial that we can't even conceive of such testimony being allowed, and secondly, I can't believe that the State even wants to put it on. If Mr. Tharp were honest, what he would say is that he is trying to use this witness to inject as much extraneous prejudicial information as he can to characterize the defendant as some kind of deviant."

The testimony about to be heard was that Diana Harrison, receptionist-secretary, had, in the course of cleaning the office one morning, noticed a wad of wet tissue in a waste can which "looked suspicious" to her. She picked it up, she said, held it to her nose and smelled it, thus determining that it was soaked with semen. Mr. Aarestad knew that Diana would further testify that after making this "discovery," she checked the appointment book for the day before and learned that a pelvic examination had indeed been performed, but not on any of the complaining witnesses. He continued his objections:

"If it is not related to a single one of these complainants, it is certainly not probative of any of the elements or allegations or charges that are before this jury. It is confusing."

But the judge disagreed.

"I am going to allow Mr. Tharp to make inquiry into this area. As I indicated before, that is provided the proper foundation is laid in this matter." What the "proper foundation" was is unclear, since Mr. Tharp then took up exactly where he left off, with the question concerning the day Diana supposedly cleaned the examining room where pelvics were given.

It was in 1983, Diana said, on a Wednesday, and what she divulged was precisely what Mr. Aarestad had feared. He continued to object, but the Court stood by its ruling and Diana's bizarre claims were allowed to stand.

She sniffed the tissue, she said, knew it was semen and from then on, suspected Dr. Story of raping his patients. Her testimony did not include, nor was it asked for, an explanation of why she had not taken her suspicions, backed up by what she now said were complaints made to her by several women, to the authorities. Neither was she asked to explain why, with what she felt was mounting evidence that Dr. Story was a rapist, did she continue to work for him and profess friendship with him and his family for another three years.

A defense witness, Dr. John E. Buster from Los Angeles, certified by the

Reproductive Interchronology Board, should been been effective in negating Diana's testimony, but for whatever reason, the jury was unimpressed. His credentials included membership in the Society for Gynecological Investigation and the American Fertility Society, so when he said that spermatozoa, or semen, cannot be identified without an "appropriate laboratory test," he should have been believed. The jury, however, may as well have yawned in his face, for all the attention they paid to his lengthy and scientific testimony concerning not only the identification of semen, but his favorable evaluation of Dr. Story's records and the procedures described therein.

Mr. Tharp's cross-examination was short, sharp and apparently effective. After a few general questions, he concluded by asking, "You are here as a consultant?" and then, "I assume the defendant has paid your way?" and "He paid you a fee to be here today?"

By this time, the California specialist was becoming impatient with the implication.

"Of course he did," he said, "My time is valuable," to which Tharp shot back, "And you were not present at the time any of the complaints were alleged to have occurred?"

Dr. Buster answered, "No, I have never been here before," and Tharp, with a satisfied smile, said, "I have nothing further."

On redirect examination, Mr. Aarestad tried to salvage his expert witness' testimony by asking, "Because you are being paid a consultant fee, would you come here and testify falsely?" to which the doctor replied firmly that he would not. The exchange was anti-climactic, however, and when he stepped from the witness stand, Dr. Buster must have wondered how much good he had really done his Wyoming colleague.

CHAPTER 30

At the conclusion of Diana Harrison's testimony, the state rested its case, court was adjourned for the day and the jury went home to ponder the strange things it had heard. Now it was defense counsel's turn, and all that remained to be seen was who would be the most believable - nine women who generally gave the impression of instability, but stuck determinedly to their stories of rape, or a group of reasonable-appearing witnesses equally determined to prove Dr. Story incapable of such actions.

It was nine o'clock the next morning, April 10, when Marilyn Story, the doctor's wife, was sworn in to testify in his behalf. Predictably, in response to Mr. Aarestad's respectful questioning, she described her thirty-two-year marriage to a gentle, sensitive man.

"We have had a very satisfying and normal, happy relationship," she said clearly, as the attorney probed carefully into the doctor's sexual practices.

"How about off-color jokes...have you ever heard him tell them?"

"No, he never speaks that way."

"Why is that?"

"He doesn't approve of such things."

"And is female privacy and modesty a

concern of his?"

"Very much so."

"Do you know where that stems from?"

"I think he is a very private person himself and he respects other people's privacy. He believes that's a right of everyone."

With her head held high and her eyes unwavering as she answered question after question, Marilyn Story gave the impression of exactly what she was - a typical Christian helpmate to her husband, assisting him in his work and sharing the family's joy and sorrow with him at home.

It is to Mr. Tharp's credit that he too, treated this courageous woman with some deference in his cross-examination and when she was allowed to step down, there were tears in many spectators' eyes. Despite her natural reticence to discuss personal matters in public, Marilyn Story knew she had been given the strength to face this latest ordeal with dignity and self-respect. As she sank gratefully into her seat, she closed her eyes and offered a silent "thank you" to her Lord and protector.

Joe Brown, Hospital Administrator at Big Horn County Memorial Hospital in Lovell, followed Marilyn in confirming her appraisal of her husband.

"He is a devoted husband and father," he said, " and his attitude in both work and in the community has always been aboveboard. No suggestive behavior, no suggestive language, nothing that would indicate any problem. In all my twenty years, he has probably one of the finest behavioral records I have ever seen."

The direct examination of Lovell's hospital administrator continued, "Do you know who the majority of the nurses in your hospital use as their physician?"

"Most of the nurses go to Dr. Story," Joe Brown replied. This seemed reassuring to the doctor's supporters and they allowed themselves a cautious moment of optimism. Surely, the jury would be impressed by this and the excellent credentials they knew were to follow. Professional colleagues and some of the town's most respected citizens would be called as character witnesses for Dr. Story.

However, only one juror, a woman, still seemed attentive to the continuing testimony - the rest appeared torpid, as if what had gone before had exhausted their ability to absorb any more information.

CHAPTER 31

Kathy and Judy Gifford are sisters-in-law, who had both worked for Dr. Story up until the time of his arrest, Kathy as a licensed practical nurse and Judy as a registered nurse.

On the day that they were to testify as character witnesses for him, they drove together to Basin and discussed again the enormity of the charges against the man they both knew to be a dedicated physician.

Both are attractive and articulate, and they hoped that what they had to offer would offset the terrible things some of his patients were saying about him. They were well-equipped to do so, Kathy having worked for him for seven years and Judy nearly five. They knew and were fond of his wife and daughters and the pain being inflicted on this close family was of great concern to them.

At Mr. Aarestad's suggestion, Kathy and Judy planned to center their testimony on professional knowledge and procedures which would blow some of the ridiculous allegations of the accusers out of the water. Accordingly, both were questioned at length by defense counsel about the reasons pelvic examinations are given, the length of time such an examination normally takes, the possibility of a discharge following a pelvic and the varying sensations a woman might experience during one. Both responded easily and Judy, in her capacity as an RN, gave detailed scientific answers.

"I knew I had done a good job," she was to say later, "but the jury just didn't listen."

Mr. Tharp's cross examination was short, in both cases. The thrust of his questioning was to show that although both of the ladies had worked closely with Dr. Story, had been his patients and had a high regard for him, they had not been in the examining room when the alleged assaults were committed. They had no defense against that type of reasoning.

At the conclusion of his interrogation, Tharp asked Judy, "so you don't know what happened or what didn't happen to them?" and she, visibly shaken, answered with tears in her eyes and voice, "Yes I do, in my heart."

CHAPTER 32

Following the professional testimony of Dr. Story's two office nurses, Mr. Aarestad introduced another registered nurse, Jackie Bischoff, who had worked with the doctor at the hospital, but had also been a patient of his since childhood.

Jackie's role was to bridge the gap between professional opinion and patient loyalty, and she was the first of a parade of exceptionally good-looking young women. It was indeed part of Aarestad's strategy to point out the incongruity of a doctor choosing to assault such a collection of unattractive females, when these beauties were equally available. Needless to say, it didn't work. Mr. Tharp continually objected to any questions regarding Dr. Story's techniques compared with other physicians and his objections were sustained by Judge Hartman.

As Kay Meeker said on Dr. Arni Burron's Denver talk show, "20-20 Insight," many months later, "the whole case was about pelvic examinations, but we were not allowed to mention the normality of his procedures or our reactions to them. I felt completely defeated and I know the other character witnesses were as frustrated as I was."

Mr. Aarestad had turned this portion of

the case over to his assistant, Scott Kath of Powell, Wyoming, and the young man began with a systematic interrogation of each of the women who had been subpoenaed to testify in Dr. Story's defense. Tharp's objections were frequent and usually sustained by the court, and after only two had testified, the judge called a bench conference. Out of hearing of the jury, he questioned Mr. Kath as to the relevance of his witnesses' statements.

"We have heard from nine victims that there was something out of the ordinary going on," Kath said, "I think we have to show that there are a number of people where this did not go on. That's the relevance. The State has paraded in front of this jury nine victims and I think it is very relevant to show that there is another story to this. In effect, there is a majority of patients, and we are not bringing them all in, but his procedures are very normal."

Tharp's next observation rendered that argument useless.

"We are not contending that he raped every woman in town," he said, "(What you are contending) is like saying that because there are more banks in town and he didn't rob all of them, he only robbed one, he is not guilty of robbing that one."

Obviously, the judge agreed. "I think we are getting into a cumulative situation. I will allow you to finish with this witness, but let's move on to something else."

As a matter of fact, five more women patients of Dr. Story's were allowed to testify briefly and several nurses who had worked with the doctor at the hospital were brought to the stand, only to suffer the same feelings of inadequacy.

Mr. Tharp seemed obsessed with letters written in support of Dr. Story in the spring and summer of 1984, many of which were printed in the Lovell Chronicle. Although the witnesses who had written such letters were candid about their reasons, - one said, "we were infuriated," - the prosecutor seemed to be trying to convey the impression that it was all part of a devious plan conceived by the doctor or his family.

Several men, pillars of the community, were called to testify to Dr. Story's reputation for morality and integrity, which they did unhesitatingly, but again, the jury was unimpressed.

Senator Cal Taggart, who many months earlier had called his friend Governor Ed Herschler, asking him to intercede for Dr. Story, was reminded of that incident during cross-examination by Prosecutor Tharp. Even though the effort had been unsuccessful, it was made to sound so corrupt, so unethical, that the normally self-confident senator stepped down feeling as thwarted as he had ever been in his life.

* * *

An astute and experienced criminal lawyer might have used entirely different tactics in the courtroom and would surely, at the very least, have insisted upon a change of venue, but in the beginning Dr. Story was adamant that his trial should take place in the county where he had friends and support, and his attorney allowed him to make that critical decision. Of all the criticisms of the doctor's defense, this one has been most frequent.

"I don't think such a phony bunch of malarkey would ever have stood up in another area," a woman wrote later to the Lovell Chronicle.

CHAPTER 33

That Dr. Story was his own worst witness is indisputable. Even he, in reflection from prison, said of himself, "I am naturally very poor at that sort of thing...I appear to be devious and not open."

The man who through the years had conducted his practice exactly as he wished, tolerating no interference or suggestion from his peers or anyone else, did so with the perfect self-confidence of the well-trained professional. He knew his abilities and his limitations, and was never reluctant to refer a patient to another physician if he felt the problem was outside of his expertise. It was this attitude toward his own and others' responsibilities which brought about the agonizing conclusion that he had been poorly served by some of his lawyers.

"Not a single lawyer properly said to me, 'Doctor, I have not handled a lot of criminal cases, but I know a good criminal defense trial lawyer who can handle this and I will see that you get to him,'" he said, "That is what every ethical physician would routinely do in a case where he is unqualified."

Unfortunately, this realization came too late, after, as the doctor says now, "I have suffered great loss and my family a greater loss."

* * *

Dr. John Story, small, neat, with the half-smile he perpetually wore in both professional and social situations, took the stand in his own defense at 10:00 a.m. on April 11. Spring was in the air and it was hard for him to believe that here in the season of Christ's resurrection, he, a life-long believer, could be fighting for his freedom in this sordid courtroom environment. That he would eventually be vindicated was still uppermost in his mind, though, as he braced himself for the examination ahead.

As Defense Counsel Aarestad laboriously led the doctor first through medical procedures which required detailed technical responses, and then through the records of each of the complaining witnesses, it became obvious that this was not the way to turn the case around. Many of the alleged incidents had supposedly happened as much as seventeen years earlier, and to expect a doctor to remember the details of an office visit that long ago was impossible. Yet neither the questioning nor the calm, inconclusive answers succeeded in conveying that fact.

The prosecutor, in his closing argument, described Dr. Story's testimony as "evasive" and accused him of having a selective memory. "He could remember what he wanted to remember - the things he didn't want to remember, he forgot," he said. That this was exactly what his own nine witnesses had done was conveniently overlooked and the jury apparently didn't make the connection either.

Defense counsel's examination of the defendant took over two hours and cross examination about an hour and a half, but compared to the droning of the defense attorney's low, monotonous voice, the prosecutor's inquiries were brisk, almost staccato. They covered the same charts, yet the jury's attention wandered during defense testimony, but picked up noticeably when Mr. Tharp began his sharp cross-examination.

His method was to keep the doctor on the defensive by asking him questions impossible to answer without looking up the answers in the charts. This Dr. Story did, dutifully counting the number of pelvic examinations given the various women and verifying the dates on which he had last seen them. He was quiet, unemotional and completely ineffective.

CHAPTER 34

When defense testimony had ended, Prosecuting Attorney Terry Tharp pulled a rabbit out of his hat.

Linda Tilley, called by the prosecution in rebuttal, was an uncharging witness. That she be allowed to testify was strongly contested by defense counsel when he said in part, "The prejudicial impact of bringing in such evidence in rebuttal at a time when the defense is not in a position to respond to it is done for the obvious purpose of prejudicing the defendant substantially."

The judge disagreed, however, and allowed the testimony with a slight concession to Mr. Aarestad. "The Court," he said, "will allow the defense a surrebuttal witness in the nature of the defendant if he desires to take the stand to rebut any testimony offered by Miss Tilley."

Linda Tilley turned out to be a married woman with four children, whose alleged experience with Dr. Story had occurred in 1971.

She claimed that "something cold" had been removed from her vagina and replaced by "something warm," and that Dr. Story had asked if she would be willing to help him. "I said 'yes' and he said 'please give me your hand.'"

"What happened from that point?" the proseuctor asked.

"He grabbed ahold of my hand and put it on himself and asked me to help him."

In cross examination, Linda recalled almost no details of the incident and admitted to doing nothing to discourage the so-called rape attempt except to say to herself (or maybe aloud, she couldn't remember) "Whoa, I'm not doing this."

"Did you kick at him or do anything to resist?" Mr. Aarestad asked.

"No."

"Did you holler, whimper or cry?"

"No."

Did you ever remove your feet from the stirrups and try to get off the table?"

"No."

"Just laid there?"

"Until he left," the witness said, and defense counsel turned his back on her.

"I think that's all we have, your Honor," he said.

It was obvious that Mr. Aarestad thought the testimony had been so ridiculous, so incredible, that it defeated the prosecution's purpose, but he may have been wrong.

As promised, however, the judge then allowed defense counsel to call Dr. Story to the stand for a terse denial of the charge.

"Any truth to that?" he asked, to which the doctor replied, "None whatsoever."

CHAPTER 35

Although Mr. Aarestad had been advised by the judge that he could call various prosecution witnesses for his "case in chief" if he so desired, he failed to do so, and in two specific instances thereby lost the opportunity to bring some pertinent information to the jury's attention in a forceful way.

Marie Fink, complainant Hayla Farwell's mother, had continued to treat with Dr. Story (including pelvic examinations) from the date of the alleged rape of her daughter in 1967 until 1983 - sixteen years - and had repeatedly taken her grandchildren (Hayla's children) to him during that time. When Aarestad attempted to bring this out in cross examination of Mrs. Fink, the prosecutor objected and the objection was sustained by the court.

"In a rape case," Aarestad said, "...cross examination... is seldom restricted unless it is completely and totally irrelevant."

"I believe the law you may be pertaining to (sic), Mr. Aarestad, may have to deal with cross-examination of the alleged victims in rape cases," Judge Hartman responded. "This is not a victim. I am going to have to go along with Mr. Tharp's argument that this is outside the scope of direct. If you wish to call this witness for your case in chief, you may certainly do so." *

"All right, we will do that," Aarestad said, but he did not. His only reference to it was in his examination of Dr. Story, when two questions, "Is Mrs. Fink a patient of yours?" and "When is the last time she visited you?" comprised the entire effort to expose this significant inconsistency.

The same was true in the case of Deanna Wagner, Gertrude Jolley's daughter, who testified for the prosecution that her mother had told her soon after the incident in 1980 that Dr. Story "raped her." Mr. Aarestad knew then that not only Deanna, but her husband, had continued as patients of Dr. Story until September of 1983, but only referred to it in the same off-hand manner in which he questioned his client about Mrs. Fink.

Spectators who were itching for some vigorous cross-examination on these and other points which to them carried so much weight in the doctor's favor, were again disappointed and confused by the seemingly casual treatment they received.

There were also lingering concerns about the failure to bring into question the credibility factor. Although the law is specific in prohibiting "reputation" evidence, it does provide a mechanism by which evidence relating to credibility may be introduced. It involves a written motion to be presented to the court ten days prior to the trial stating that the defense has an "offer of proof of the relevancy of evidence of the sexual conduct of the victim and its relevancy to the defense."

Considering the information Mr. Aarestad had about the nine prosecution witnesses prior to the trial, everyone who wanted Dr. Story's case to be handled in the most effective manner felt cheated that none of it had come out in court.

As a matter of fact, researchers who have reviewed pre-trial motions do not believe that the defense ever presented the necessary paperwork. A question specifically directed to Aarestad regarding this following the trial brought the answer that it was not the law governing sexual assault, but Wyoming's "Rules of Evidence" that precluded his using the documented evidence he had to impeach the credibility of the complaining witnesses.

It would take another lawyer experienced in sexual assault cases to fully determine where the fault lay, but the fact remains that information so critical to Dr. Story's defense never reached the jury's ears.

To compound the problem, even though there is some discretion allowed the court in this area, Judge Gary Hartman was known to be stern about introducing "reputation evidence," according to the prosecuting attorney.

In one of Tharp's interviews with a prospective witness against Dr. Story, he assured her, "the fact that these things may have happened to you in the past, unless they can somehow show that you are in the habit of making false accusations, those things aren't going to be allowed by a judge, **not the judge we have, anyway.**"

Neither did the favorable results of psychological and lie detector tests Dr.

Story underwent prior to his trial, become known. To spectators whose only background in law was watching criminal trial lawyers at work on television, this omission seemed to be an error on the part of defense counsel. Questions on the subject were not clearly answered and no one really wanted to imply that more experience and aggressiveness on the part of Dr. Story's attorney might have made the difference between victory and defeat.

Dr. Story himself, though, after a few months' access to the prison law library, concluded that his legal representation had been "expensive and useless," and told a friend later, "I know it is not as hard for patients, even those without money, to find good, committed doctors who will fight for their patients' health and life, as it is for clients to find a similarly disposed lawyer."

* When the Supreme Court, fourteen months later, overturned Dr. Story's conviction in Hayla Farwell's case, Judge Hartman's action in disallowing cross examination of Marie Fink was one of the reasons.

"The Court obviously realized that this line of cross-examination was relevant," they wrote, "because the Court suggested that defense counsel raise the issue in its case in chief. This procedure does not cure the Court's error. Defense counsel should not be forced to call a witness back to the stand later in the case in order to attack (her) credibility. If a witness's misstatements are not demonstrated immediately, they can color the jury's view of the other evidence which follows. Defense counsel's eventual attack on the witness's credibility may come too late."

CHAPTER 36

Prosecuting Attorney Terry Tharp, flamboyant in a plaid sport coat and flushed with the success of his aggressive cross-examination of Dr. Story, approached his closing argument with confidence.

This was the biggest case he had ever handled and whether or not he intended to expand his activities outside Big Horn County, its successful outcome couldn't help but be good for his career. So far, things had gone even better than he expected and he felt sure that he could cinch the guilty verdict with a few well-turned phrases repeated enough times.

Overzealous prosecutors can be found on every level of the judicial system and the Fifth Judicial District in Wyoming is no exception.*

Tharp's only well-grounded argument was that Dr. Story and each of the nine accusers had been alone in the examining room at the time of the alleged incidents.** This was incontrovertible and no one on the defense team had even tried to deny it. In fact, the women patients who had been allowed to testify in the doctor's behalf were prepared to state strongly that they either didn't care or actually preferred not to have a third person in the examining room.

Otherwise, the prosecutor's contentions that the women were all placed in a "vulnerable position," (the **only** position in which a pelvic examination is performed), that they were "draped so they couldn't see," (the **only** way in which the modesty of a patient is protected) and that the doctor "stood between their legs" (the **only** way any doctor can accomplish the manual portion of a pelvic examination) were like so much lint floating around the courtroom.

Two statements were false. Hayla Farwell, he said, was "never pursued for her bill," when according to Hayla's court testimony, she paid her bill after she was threatened with collection.

Emma McNeil never claimed to have seen a penis, but in his zeal to convince his audience, the prosecutor said that she did. Probably neither of these mistakes made much difference in the outcome of the trial, but they show the determination to win which overshadowed the desire for accuracy.

The rest of the prosecution's closing argument dealt solely with the word of nine highly volatile witnesses against that of one morally upright and emotionally stable man who had nothing to gain and everything to lose by the actions of which he was accused.

One by one, Tharp briefly reviewed the nine cases, emphasizing that each woman "felt a penis," or "saw a penis." Thus, the baffling circumstances surrounding these episodes and the absence of any real evidence were successfully buried in the pile of fluff settling on his one valid point - no third party could come forward and say, "I was there and it didn't happen!"

* At the top of the scale are two government officials, James M. Beggs, administrator of the National Aeronautics and Space Administration (NASA) and Ray Donovan, Secretary of Labor in the Reagan administration.

These two innocent men, although they were both acquitted in the end, came out of their legal ordeals financially ruined, with their reputations blackened forever. Both indictments were condemned by the "Wall Street Journal" as flagrant examples of "prosecutorial indiscretion."

** The one exception was Wanda Hammond, whose chart showed that her appointment was for the insertion of an IUD, a procedure requiring the presence of a nurse. Defense counsel, however, failed to produce that nurse and Wanda denied ever having an IUD inserted by Dr. Story. This allegedly perjurious denial was many months later the object of an appeal for a new trial by Dr. Story, which was refused by the court.

CHAPTER 37

Defense counsel, by contrast, seemed low-key and sluggish. Mr. Aarestad, whose voice and manner were far from commanding, said the right things in the wrong way. His opening paragraphs were scholarly and courteous, thanking the jury for their attention throughout the trial and stressing the importance of a carefully deliberated verdict. "Sometimes in the determination of truth," he said, "you have to go down deep into yourself for individual wisdom and deep into yourselves collectively as a jury."

It was mid-morning when Mr. Aarestad began his closing argument. He too, went case by case through the preceding testimony, pointing out inconsistencies and some of the incredible information presented. His primary contention was that Dr. Story was "practicing nineteenth century medicine in the twentieth century."

"His sin," he said, "was the failure to practice medicine with a law book in his back pocket. He trusted his patients...He said, 'if my patients are concerned with modesty and privacy and don't want a third person in there during an intimate examination, I'll honor that even though there are risks that incur to me.' The entire testimony shows that Dr. Story was one hundred percent patient oriented. Not person oriented. To a fault. And that's really why he is here today. Had he practiced medicine with a law book in his back pocket he wouldn't be here. But to take that piece of information and stretch it to a conclusion and inference that the State would have you adopt and accept that because he did not have a third person in there somehow equates to guilt, is in my opinion, absurd. That's a big leap."*

He pleaded with the jury not to be "confused by numbers", at one point referring to the prosecution's case as a "shotgun approach."

"In other words," he said, "drum up as many alleged victims as you can, throw as much mud against the wall as you can and hope that a little bit sticks. One conviction is as bad as all of them." and

"The purpose that caused the State to go looking for alleged victims, you will recall the testimony that it was the police that contacted them, not the other way around, is because they want to confuse quantity with quality. What they lack in quality, hard solid evidence for a conviction, they want to make up by throwing numbers at you...number of victims, number of exams, amount of time it takes..."

These were all strong arguments, as were:

"What you will see is that somebody, and it is not his responsibility to prove, somebody either wants Dr. Story out of Lovell or wants him out of practice, but is out to get him." and

"In his opening statement, Mr. Tharp promised you that he was going to call nurses, secretaries and receptionists that had worked for Dr. Story to establish their case. They offer you up Diana Harrison, a receptionist...and Pam Mayer, a non-medically trained person who worked for him a couple of months more than a decade ago whose daughter is one of the complainants and they say these are our nurses, secretaries and receptionists. On the other hand, we offered secretaries, receptionists and nurses...who go back over 20 years...as an unbroken chain of testimony as to the consistency of his practice, his protocol, his procedures and everything."

In fairness to Mr. Aarestad, a reading of his complete closing argument shows fine preparation and a recognition of the salient points of the case. The problem was in delivery.

Just before court was adjourned for a lunch break, defense counsel gave what should have stirred the jury to some genuine soul-searching.

"I want you to get into just how deep that type of an assault would produce outrage," he said. "And then take a look at some of the testimony. One thanks the doctor on her way out. One stops at the front desk and pays a bill. Some come back, continue to use him as their physician. I think when you weigh those factors you will see and know and realize that those types of responses are inconsistent with human nature and that goes to the credibility of their testimony...There was substantial testimony that they didn't trust the legal environment because who would believe them. It would be simply their word against somebody else's. Weigh that response in respect to this outrage. And why all of a sudden, years later, they all seem to not have that problem any more and now they trust the legal environment. It miraculously disappeared in each one of their cases, coincidentally at the same time. Ponder some of those things. It will help explain why they are here. In that respect their numbers defeat them."

The jury members looked blank as they gratefully filed out for their mid-day meal.

*Throughout the Story's ordeal, unsolicited testimonials to the doctor's high moral standards have come to the family and the defense committee.

Nellie Snyder Yost, Nebraska author, says of him, "His own decency and trust brought about his downfall."

Another, from Theodor Bernardy, M.D. of Springfield, Illinois, describes Dr. Story's character as "honorable, decent, responsible and dedicated to his profession and his family."

CHAPTER 38

It was 1:30 on April 16, 1985, another unseasonably warm day, when court re-adjourned for the final arguments in Dr. Story's behalf. There was restlessness on both sides - the prosecution wanting to get it over with and defense supporters wanting Mr. Aarestad to attack - to demand the jury's attention and finally, to clear his client's name with some sweeping, combative rhetoric that would end this nightmare. Again they were disappointed. The attorney kept doggedly to his notes, rehashing defense testimony and trying to discredit the "expert" testimony of Dr. Flory. Then, without warning, the judge declared, "Mr. Aarestad, you have two minutes left."

Unfair? The stunned audience had never heard of such a thing, but Mr. Aarestad didn't seem surprised. He thanked the judge and quickly concluded his closing argument. It was not learned until later that at the noon recess, the judge had asked Mr. Aarestad how much longer he thought his closing argument would be. Aarestad replied that it should be about an hour and then amended that to forty-five minutes. Right or wrong, the judge was simply reminding defense counsel that his estimated time was nearly up.

Prosecutor Tharp was allowed a final rebuttal and he took advantage of it to regale the jury one more time with "numbers, numbers, numbers. His opening statement was crude and unreasonable, but probably effective.

"I want to counter a few of the cheap shots, the insinuations, the distortions and misstatements made in that final argument," he said.

Months later, Dr. Story's new attorney, Gerald Mason, referred to this in Dr. Story's appeal to the Wyoming Supreme Court.

"...for whatever purpose and reason, he (Tharp) repeatedly elected to resort to a violation of professional standards to obtain the conviction of appellant," he wrote, "Perhaps his attitude is best illustrated by an unprofessional remark appearing in the rebuttal argument," and Mason quoted verbatim Tharp's opening statement.

"Those kinds of opinions," he added, "if held by the prosecutor, should be kept to himself, not argued to the jury, especially in a rebuttal argument where the defense has no opportunity even to respond."

But Attorney Tharp was unrestrained as he made his final plea for conviction of the defendant and his closing statement, while not profound, was effective.

" Just remember one thing as you go back in there to deliberate," he said, "Be very careful, very careful of the words of anybody who finds himself in a perilous position."

And then it was over. Wayne Aarestad had done his best and had concluded his argument with an entreaty to God to bless the jury and give them wisdom, but his words fell on barren ground. A day and a half later, the jury brought in a verdict of guilty on six counts. Aarestad's pleas for "the test of reason" to be applied to the testimony they had heard had been ignored and now all that remained was the sentencing of the man who thought he was invulnerable.

CHAPTER 39

The sentencing of Dr. John H. Story, convicted of raping or attempting to rape his female patients over a period of eighteen years, took place on June 8, 1985.

Between April 16, when the trial ended and the beautiful early summer day when sentence was passed, Dr. Story had been held first in Big Horn County jail in Basin and then Park County jail in Cody. Both are within an hour's drive from Lovell, so Marilyn could visit him whenever the rules allowed. Their times together were distinguished from other prisoners and their wives by prayer and their deep and abiding faith that they were still held securely in God's hand.

After his conviction, Dr. Story's enemies, particularly unbelievers, thought he was finally down and anticipated a bloody finish.

The press, after its day-by-day coverage of the longest and most sensational trial ever held in Big Horn County, was reluctant to turn loose, and hurried to ask the imprisoned doctor how he felt about his conviction. Readers of that first interview were either inspired or deflated by Dr. Story's comment that "This is where faith comes in - I am no different now than a week ago."

Those who had hoped to see a broken man pleading for mercy were disappointed, but his friends, who knew the depth of his beliefs, were not surprised.

At home, the Dr. Story Defense Committee had officially been formed and had submitted petitions and letters supporting Dr. Story to Judge Gary Hartman.

"We would ask the Court's indulgence in letting (Dr. Story) out on bail, as we feel he is not now, or ever has been a threat to the community," they said in a cover letter written May 8, 1985. "We implore you to release the doctor, as we still believe in his professional and moral integrity." It was signed by the officers of the group, Jan Hillman,Chairman; Wes Meeker, Vice-Chairman; Kay Meeker, Secretary; and members Ralph Fink, R. C. Richardson, Polly Boggess, Tom Mulford and Steve Miller.

Behind them were the majority of Lovell residents, many of whom were vocal in their loyalty and anxious for an opportunity to help in some way.

Although their efforts at that time had no effect on the Judge's decision, their enthusiasm was successfully channeled in the months to come, and by December, various fund-raising events had produced nearly $20,000 to be used in the doctor's continuing defense.

Shortly after the trial, a ray of hope appeared. The pre-sentencing investigation was to be done by a Cody probation officer, Paul Sironen, and after his first contact with members of the Defense Committee, they felt that here might be someone at last who would take an objective look at the other side of the story.

In their meeting with him, Jan, Wes and Kay provided Sironen with a wealth of information about the investigative methods, reputations of the accusers and names of more people to contact. At the conclusion, they felt good about what his investigation might bring out, but their optimism was short-lived. It soon became obvious that he was spending most of his time with the same people who had brought about Dr. Story's downfall, and from them had heard of even more women who "thought they might have been" assaulted by their physician. The committee was later to complain formally to the State Executive Director of the Department of Probation and Parole.

"We demand an accounting of such negligent behavior on the part of Mr. Sironen," they wrote, "An investigation is just that, an investigation, not a repetition of prosecutorial rhetoric. If this is the best your department can do, the State of Wyoming is wasting its tax dollars."

The committee further requested a meeting with the Director to "discuss your departmental investigative procedures," but their request was denied.

Another, even more strongly worded letter was directed to Judge Hartman following Dr. Story's sentencing. On July 15, 1985, the Dr. Story Defense Committee wrote that "at his request (Paul Sironen) was given a list of approximately 120 random patient names and was told 200 or more could be furnished if he so desired. We also provided him with names of women who were questioned during the initial investigation by Judi Cashel, but had given favorable statements about Dr. Story and therefore had their statements destroyed by Ms. Cashel as not pertinent to the case. Mr. Sironen was also given copies of letters written on behalf of Dr. Story and petitions with over 800 names of supporters.

"With all of (the) information available to him, Paul Sironen chose not to contact any of these people. Nor did he contact any members of the hospital staff, some of whom had worked with Dr. Story for over twenty-five years. How could he possibly present an even remotely accurate picture of Dr. Story's history without interviewing persons who knew him best and worked with him in his professional environment, the environment in which he has been found guilty of various crimes?"

They concluded, "Mr. Sironen's lack of consideration in providing Dr. Story and the Defense with a copy of the report only hours before the sentencing is exemplary of his behavior throughout the entire investigation. In your (Judge Hartman's) own statement, you said you had the opportunity to study the report thoroughly. The Defense did not. Had the Defense had the opportunity to review the report with Mr. Sironen, the voluminous errors could have been corrected by him. For a man who came to us saying he wanted a large number of people to contact in order to gain the true picture regarding Dr. Story, Paul Sironen greatly limited his search for truth by primarily dealing with those involved in the prosecution."

This was submitted for the Court's record, where it lay apparently unnoticed, or at least unavailing.

Another crippling blow had been dealt the doctor.

CHAPTER 40

At the sentencing, Mr. Aarestad tried unsuccessfully to persuade Judge Hartman to remove himself as the sentencing judge, arguing that Mr. Sironen's information regarding uncharging victims was, by his own acknowledgment, hearsay.

"We do not believe," Aarestad said, "that the Court can separate this prejudicial information from the convictions upon which the Court must base its decision concerning sentencing."

Judge Hartman replied that in going over the pre-sentence investigation "very, very carefully," he had noted that the sections of the report entitled, "Prior Offenses" and "Victim Impact," were without doubt based on hearsay and that he (the Court) certainly "cannot and does not take that into consideration."

In other words, the Judge declared himself competent to separate fact from hearsay, denied the motion to remove himself from the sentencing procedure and the hearing moved ahead.

Perhaps some of the most powerful and moving testimony of the entire trial was given on that day. Called to the stand were Dr. Story's aged mother, his sister, his two daughters and his wife, and these five devoted women pled for leniency with all of the eloquence born of love and complete confidence.

At age eighty-five, Inez Story was firm in her belief in her son's innocence and her judgment of his accusers.

"I think a man so interested in the welfare of others, who has given the best of his life to the people up here for the good of the community - it would seem almost impossible that they would want to destroy his life. They have ruined it and that of his family and ruined him financially and his medical practice and disrupted his home. It is time for some justice in this community. I believe many lies have been told here to destroy him."*

Gretchen Stevens, the doctor's sister, was calm, dignified and clear in her description of her brother's station in life.

"He is the role model for my family," she said with head held high, "I think he is the role model for many people but in particular for my son who is going into medicine. We all respect him highly. We are all aware of his devotion to the scriptures. He believes them wholeheartedly and lives what he believes."

Susan, John and Marilyn's older daughter, demure, soft-spoken, but as determined as the rest to defend her father in whatever way left open to her, found it hard to express her feelings adequately.

"I feel so frustrated because words cannot describe what kind of person he is and what it is like to live with him. I feel I have the most wonderful mother and father that anyone could have. He has been a richness in my life and I just can't explain it."

She did explain it well, however, as she detailed her work as a registered nurse in the same hospital where her father practiced.

"Over the past six years," she said, "I have worked in three different hospitals and I have seen a number of doctors and I also had the privilege of working with my father and was able to see him in actual, real life practice of medicine. I can testify that he is a rare doctor. Not many doctors show the respect for the individual that he does."

Marilyn, by now worn and haggard by the lengthy trial and the forced separation from her husband she had endured since the conviction, reiterated some of the things she had said in her original testimony. But in closing her entreaty for his freedom pending appeal of the conviction, she said what every friend, relative, patient and co-worker of Doc's felt in his or her heart.

"I have always had great trust in our judicial system," she said, her voice breaking slightly, "but now I know that innocent men go to prison...He is the victim...These false accusations have totally ruined our lives. He has already paid way too high a price for this."

As she left the stand, hands and hearts reached out to her, but her agony was, for the moment, untouchable by human compassion.

Linda Story, the youngest member of the family, should have been the last to testify, as her plea would have made an appropriate finale to the whole production.

"I know that through all of this," she said, "my dad's greatest concern has been for the welfare of the family and of my mother in particular. And he is her only means of support, therefore I would desire that the Court suspend his sentence in order that he might continue to care for her. I am convinced that he is totally innocent, not just because he is my father but because I know his character, his stability, his dedication to God and his principles..."

"My father has taught me to value God-given life, to value people and to value a day or an hour spent in the sun. And to deny him his quality of life and to deny him and my mother their later years together greatly compounds the injustice that has been done to him by this Court."

Tears flowed freely from the eyes of men and women alike, as Linda, small, resolute and looking very much like her father, spoke directly to the judge.

* "At the sentencing of Dr. Story, there were several dozen of his supporters from Lovell carrying picket signs. One of the signs read, '50 Lies Don't Make One Truth,' but fifty lurid, exciting lies, repeated many times, did win over the dull, boring truth that NOTHING HAPPENED. Who cares?" Howard I. Story, Maxwell, Nebraska

CHAPTER 41

If Judge Hartman was moved by Dr. Story's family's pleas in his behalf, it was unnoticeable as he rendered his decision concerning the sentence to be served and the question of bail pending appeal of the conviction.

The words were right, as he acknowledged the doctor's "age, intelligence, training, background, lack of criminal record and present attitude."

He had also considered, he said, "the number of lives that you must have saved in Lovell, the many calls that a physician is called upon to make at all hours of the day, the number of persons you have healed and those you have treated and those persons that you have been both a counselor and a confidant for."

But, he went on, "I have also considered the number of crimes for which you have been convicted numbering six...I have also considered the psychological and emotional havoc you have visited upon those victims. And I'm certain that the scars you so inflicted cannot measure, by any stretch of the imagination, any type of sentence that I could impose."

"A judge, when he considers sentencing," Hartman continued, "should consider...the possibility for rehabilitation. The Court notes that there has been no admission by you that any of those crimes have occurred. Also the Court has taken into consideration the question of whether or not any incarceration would deter the general public from committing these types of crimes or specific persons from committing these crimes. The Court has also considered the factor of incapacitation, whether you need to be separated from society. And finally, the Court has considered the question of retribution, that one who breaks the law must pay the penalty or receive his just deserves (sic)."

Whereupon, sentences of terms from fifteen to twenty years in prison, to run concurrently, were handed down on six of the nine cases.

The finishing touch was a denial of bail on appeal and Dr. Story was led away, ashen and tight-lipped, but still calm in the strength of his great faith. His womenfolk too, held up until the courtroom was emptied of spectators before falling into one another's arms in utter despair.

"It was the worst day of our lives," Susan was to say later. "Somehow, to the very end, we thought it couldn't really happen and then it did."

CHAPTER 42

Despite what some felt was Wayne Aarestad's closest brush with eloquence in the entire trial, Judge Hartman denied bail with no explanation. If he felt that Dr. Story was a poor flight risk, he did not say so and his sentencing covered all other aspects of the case.*

Aarestad had pleaded well for two possibilities - preferably a suspended sentence but at least, release on bail pending appeal. He stressed the doctor's character - "He does not pose an unreasonable risk to flee which is the purpose for bail consideration," he said.

"I believe that Dr. Story would have left long ago if he had been guilty of these charges," he continued, "and I believe that he is going to see through the appellate process and whatever is necessary for an ultimate vindication of what has occurred here. There is nothing in his past to suggest that he would run. There is no indication that he would abandon this community, abandon his family, abandon friends who mean so terribly much to him...He has never been one to run from any conflict, from any battle."

In his last-ditch effort to avert disaster, Aarestad also reminded the court that although his license had still not been formally revoked, the doctor had voluntarily surrendered it as a gesture of assurance that he would no longer be functioning in the environment in which the charges of sexual misconduct had occurred.

"There is no hint by virtue of any evidence submitted during the course of the trial," Aarestad said, "that Dr. Story poses a threat to anybody outside of a medical environment, and he has removed himself from that environment...(He) is in no position to practice medicine, has no intention of practicing medicine...(and) does not pose any type of hazard to society by any reasonable evidence presented to this Court."

The desperate attorney, in the face of overwhelming odds, determinedly recited once more the facts of Dr. Story's value to the community and dedication to his practice.

"He provided a continuity of medical services for the North Big Horn County region that was not there. Largely due to his efforts and his presence, there is a hospital in Lovell. There is a high quality of medical care available because of this man's ceaseless dedication in his profession. It is a terrible tragedy, it is a terrible waste of human life, it is a terrible travesty of justice to witness... I don't know that at this point there is any (way) this Court can undo what has already been done. However, we believe that either a suspended sentence or a release on bail pending completion of the appeal is a reasonable request...We think that would be a demonstrative act of justice and certainly justifiable under the circumstances. We would seek that lenience from the Court today."

When he sat down, there was an almost imperceptible stir in the courtroom, as if friend and foe alike were bracing for the final blow.

The judge turned to the defendant and asked, "John Story, do you have anything you would like to say to the Court prior to passing sentence in this case?" And the doctor, to whom the use of his given name without the title "Dr." was an intolerable impertinence, answered stiffly, "I think not."

"Is there any reason why sentence should not be pronounced at this time?"

Again, characteristically stoic, the doctor replied, "I am aware of none," and stood defiantly as the life he had known for fifty-eight years was pronounced finished.

The rest is Big Horn County history. Sentence was passed, bail denied and newspaper reporters flew to telephone their editors of the climax of the two-month-long ordeal. It was over, finished, and no way, the "victims" said to one another, would he ever be free again.

Indeed, in those first black days after Doc was taken first to the state mental hospital in Evanston, Wyoming for evaluation and then to the state penitentiary in Rawlins, it did seem that there was nothing more to do.

*Later, when a motion to set bail was argued by defense counsel, Judge Hartman responded with the explanation that before the conviction, he felt Dr. Story was sure he would be acquitted and for that reason, made all his court appearances. Now that he is convicted, he said, the risk of flight would be very high.

CHAPTER 43

Wayne Aarestad, who had spoken so confidently of a successful appeal, seemed to fade from the picture and the next thing Doc's supporters knew was that two new attorneys from Pinedale, Wyoming, had taken over the case.

Gerald Mason, heavy-set and somber, but quick of mind and manner, was the lead lawyer, with his partner, Van Graham as back-up. Their first act was to initiate proceedings to get the doctor out of jail on bond and on Friday, August 16, 1985, they were successful. It was a masterful move on the part of Mr. Mason, who chose to seek relief from Judge Hartman's decision in the jurisdiction of District Court Judge Robert Hill in Rawlins.

When word of the doctor's impending release filtered out early in the week, the State Attorney General's office hastily moved to block the action by asking the Supreme Court to overturn Hill's ruling. They were too late, though - Mason had flown the Judge's order to the penitentiary immediately after a $50,000 bond was posted, and less than two hours later, Dr. John Story walked out of the penitentiary a temporarily free man.

This generated some hate mail for Judge

Hill and a cartoon in the Casper Star Tribune which was deplored by Dr. Story's supporters and no doubt applauded by his detractors. (Illustration)

Sylvia Hackl, who would later represent the State in Dr. Story's appeal to the Wyoming Supreme Court, spoke to reporters following the release.

"They (Supreme Court judges) obviously didn't act to delay the release," she said. "Now what we're doing is waiting. What we do next is based on what, if any, decision the Supreme Court makes and we have no indication of when that might be."

Mrs. Hackl added that she believed the court could still act to return the doctor to prison but they did not, and in March 1986 ruled that Judge Hill was correct in his decision to allow Dr. Story to return home pending the appeal of his case.

Big Horn County Attorney Terry Tharp, who had prosecuted the doctor, was not happy with the decision, but said he would "have to live with it."

"I'm concerned about possible consequences to him, too," he added, "You're dealing with some pretty highly charged emotions."

Tharp needn't have worried. Dr. and Marilyn Story took up their quiet life much as it had been before the trial, with one major exception. Although Doc went to his hilltop clinic almost daily, the rooms were empty of patients and the space he and Marilyn were able to clear of equipment and records was rented to a new doctor in Lovell. Doc's hours spent in those familiar surroundings were the necessary ones to close a practice, and put behind him

Printed in August 1985, following Doc's release on bond

twenty-six years of service to a community.

At Christmas, the Defense Committee put out the third issue of "The Real Story," the newsletter designed to keep supporters up to date on progress in the case. At that time, they advised that attorneys Mason and Graham had completed the written appeal and filed it with the Supreme Court.

"They will appear before the Court some time in December or January," they said, "to give the oral presentation." They also reported that the costs of the appeal process alone, up to that time, had totalled over $29,000, $19,000 of which the committee had been able to pay, "thanks to contributors," they said.

Doc and Marilyn also added personal messages to their friends far and near, which they began with an anonymous quotation.

"The Lord may not have planned that this should overtake me, but He has most certainly permitted it. Therefore, though it were an attack of an enemy, by the time it reaches me, it has the Lord's permission and therefore all is well. He will make it work together with all life's experiences for good."

Again, Doc and Marilyn tried to reassure their friends as they themselves faced the most devastating period of their lives.

CHAPTER 44

Later in March 1986, after the Supreme Court had upheld Judge Robert Hill's decision to release Dr. Story on bail, the Lovell anti-Doc forces mustered enough strength to have him hauled back to court.

Senior Assistant to the Wyoming Attorney General, Sylvia Hackl, filed a petition in Judge Hill's Rawlins court to revoke the doctor's bail, stating that while Dr. Story was not seeing patients, he was involved in the practice of medicine.

The reasoning seemed faulty. Dr. Story, the petition stated, was using an office in the back of the medical clinic (which he owned), had a sign on his office reading "John H. Story, M.D.," and answered the phone there with "Dr. Story's office."

These factors, according to Mrs. Hackl, constitute the practice of medicine as outlined in the state statutes. Lovell witnesses were on hand to testify to these alleged infractions of the law.

Attorney Mason refuted the claims by pointing out that after twenty-six years in the practice of medicine in Lovell, the doctor would normally have paper work to clear up and would understandably "kill time" in those familiar surroundings.

Marilyn also confirmed that Doc spent

time in the office reading medical journals.

As for the use of the title, "Dr. or M.D.," the doctor himself testified that his doctorate in medicine had not, nor could it be, revoked, only his license to practice medicine, which he maintained he was not doing.

Judge Hill denied the petition and Doc remained free on bail for another three months. A spring edition of the "The Real Story" carried an article questioning the State's action.

"We wonder," it read, "why Doc was harrassed in this way and what the costs were to the county for this ridiculous court action. The court has jurisdiction over licensing, but a question arises when the legal system attempts to take away his doctor's degree. Practicing medicine is seeing patients, not having 'M.D.' after your name."

This was a layman's opinion, of course, but it did make a good point with regard to the expensive nit-picking the state resorted to in an effort to speed Dr. Story's return to prison.

CHAPTER 45

On December 17, 1985, the Wyoming Supreme Court's capital city courtroom was packed with "one of the largest spectator audiences ever," Wyoming State Tribune editor James Flinchum wrote in the lead article in his Cheyenne-based newspaper.

The occasion was Dr. John Story's appeal, at which his attorneys asked the Supreme Court to overturn the Lovell physician's six counts of rape conviction.

Doc and Marilyn were not present, but Susan, who was living and working in Ft. Collins, Colorado by that time, was in the audience, flanked by an uncle and two good friends now living in Cheyenne.

Characteristic of the family, she maintained superb control throughout the proceedings, but wrote later, "It's still so hard to believe that I was sitting in the State Supreme Court room hearing my dad's name spoken in that way."

Although the news media stressed only one point of the appeal - deprivation of the appellant's constitutional right to due process of law by the delayed prosecution - the eighty-eight-page brief contained eleven "statements of the issue on appeal."

The first was, as reported, "The extensive precharging delay deprived appellant of due process of law, but the ten following were equally revealing of error.

2) The trial court erred in admitting, without appropriate foundation, evidence of an out-of-court experiment, (Dr. Flory) 3) The trial court erred in admitting evidence of a tissue allegedly containing semen where such was unrelated to any complaint, 4) The appellant was deprived of a fair trial by the evidentiary rulings of the trial court, 5) The state was guilty of prosecutorial misconduct, 6) The state erroneously interfered with appellant's cross-examination of state's witnesses, 7) The trial court erroneously restricted appellant in presenting evidence relevant to the theory of his defense, 8) The trial court erred in admitting the testimony of a non-charging witness on rebuttal, 9) The limits placed on appellant's surrebuttal by the trial court was an abuse of discretion, 10) The trial court erred in its instructions to the jury and 11) The conviction on count II of the information for the first degree rape of Terri Timmons was not supported by sufficient evidence.

The number of issues in the appeal made it unwieldy, and Attorney Mason apologized to the court at the conclusion of his oral argument.

"Appellant appreciates the patience required to reach this point in the Argument and Brief. Appellant has raised and argued eleven issues on appeal. Ordinarily that is too many. It is difficult for the Court to deal with eleven issues in a single appeal and give each of them the kind of careful consideration they should receive.

"Further," he said, "appellant is aware

that ordinarily eleven issues are raised only if the appellant does not have a 'good' issue and is using a 'shotgun' approach hoping the cumulative effect of all will overcome the weakness of each. While that may be true in an ordinary case, it is decidedly not true here."

Mr. Mason continued, "This was not a clean trial and the record is full of error. There is not a single weak issue in the whole appeal. The Court needs to have the opportunity on this appeal to review carefully and meticulously each one of these issues because of their individual merit."

Mr. Mason himself was meticulous, and in his conclusion he wrote, "The appellant was not accorded his procedural rights. He was not given his day in court. Though there are those that would find the results to their satisfaction, they are not just results, because they were not obtained by just means. We dare not abandon our insistence on adherence to just means. This case must be reversed."

On June 17, 1986, Dr. and Marilyn Story were notified by their attorney that one charge of assault and battery with intent to rape, brought by Hayla Farwell, had been overturned, but the Supreme Court Justices upheld the trial court's judgment on the other five counts.

It was a bitter disappointment to everyone in the Story camp, and the doctor himself said grimly, when he heard the news, "It is what I expected - they have thrown me a crumb."

CHAPTER 46

Noting "erroneous assumptions" found in the Supreme Court's decision, Dr. Story's attorneys quickly filed a new petition for "rehearing and for a correction of, or addition to, the record by way of affidavits." This petition pointed out several occurrences during the trial in April 1985 that did not appear in the trial record reviewed by the justices of the Supreme Court.

The hearing was denied and Dr. Story was ordered back to the state prison in Rawlins. According to the Defense Committee newsletter, "The Real Story," dated October 1986, "There was a flurry of excitement as County Attorney Terrill Tharp raced to Cody to get Judge Dixon to sign the papers so the doctor could be picked up (for return to prison). Probably the prosecutor had visions of putting the doctor in chains, cuffs and leg irons to transport him back to the prison with great show, as they had done before. When notified, Mr. Mason communicated with the judge by telephone and Judge Dixon didn't see that an arrest-like termination of bail was necessary."

Dr. John Story re-entered the Wyoming State Penitentiary on August 4, 1986, and this time there was the sound of finality as his cell door closed behind him.

CHAPTER 47

When Dr. Story was safely behind bars again, it was expected that his "victims" would fade quietly and gratefully into the background and try to resume a normal life. Not so. Early in 1986, several of them were interviwed by a writer from "Ladies Home Journal," for a piece published in June of that year, entitled, "Doctors, Patients and Sex."

Although Dr. Story and his patients who claimed to have been raped by him were the lead story in the article, no details whatsoever were given. Readers were not told that the women had, at the time of the alleged incidents, only "suspected" or "thought" something improper had happened. Neither was anything said about how the assaults were said to have been accomplished.

Most women, reading such an article, would assume that intercourse took place in a more or less traditional position, and under some restraint by the doctor. Had the writer described the scenario where their physician placed them in the standard position for a gynecological examination, stood between their legs in the accepted manner, performed the usual manual exam and then, with no preliminary word or action, inserted his fully erect penis in their vaginas, it would have changed the whole picture. So would their admissions that they had made no outcry or attempt to get away and that in some cases, after the alleged assault, they either returned to the doctor themselves, or continued to take their children to him.

The article did not deal solely with Dr. Story. It included quotes from a number of other women who said their doctors had assaulted them in some way, but the Lovell physician with multiple charges against him was the centerpiece.

At the end, the writer offered some "warning signs," all but one of which dealt with signals every one of his alleged victims said were never given. 1) Flattery and/or fondling, 2) "Sexy" conversation and/or dirty jokes, and 3) unnecessary house calls and/or making appointments himself rather than leaving it to his secretary.

The only "warning sign" which could conceivably be applied to Dr. Story's supposed "modus operandi" was that of the doctor who doesn't have a nurse present during the examination. Even the effectiveness of that warning was somewhat diluted by the final sentence.

"Be aware," it cautioned, "that the presence of a nurse doesn't guarantee safety," and went on to state that in one case a doctor had molested a patient while his nurse was busy taking notes in the background!

Supporters wrote the magazine protesting the article and suggesting that there was more to the Story story if reporter Rita

Rooney cared to follow it up, but a man convicted of rape, regardless of what anyone says about his innocence, does not generate sympathy and there was no response to their letters.

Now, surely, the nine charging witnesses would subside, everyone thought, but again, they were wrong.

In late August of the same year, word was passed around Lovell that ten women would appear on the Oprah Winfrey show in September. It was not the "gang of nine" who had testifed against Dr. Story in court, but a curious mix.

Four of them were prosecution witnesses of whose charges the doctor had been found guilty, Emma Lu Meeks, Annella St. Thomas, Terri Timmons and Wanda Hammond.

The fifth was Aletha Durtsche, whose story of repeated rape by her doctor was not believed by the jury, and the sixth was Hayla Farwell, whose case had been overturned by the Wyoming Supreme Court.

Three others were Meg Anderson, Minda Brinkerhoff and Minda's mother-in-law, Dorothy Brinkerhoff, none of whom were prosecution witnesses at the criminal trial.

The tenth participant was Diana Harrison, the receptionist who claimed to have "sniffed out" the evidence that her boss was raping his patients.

The group was accompanied by their old friend, Judi Cashel, ostensibly there to bolster their courage.*

Oprah opened by acknowledging that she had learned about the case from the "Ladies Home Journal," and from then on, it was a mock courtroom scene, where Oprah, as the prosecuting attorney, drew the same stories from six of the same witnesses. Three others, whose testimony had originally been classified as lacking credibility and probably harmful to the case, were also allowed to describe their experiences, and Diana Harrison repeated her bizarre account of the wet tissue in the trash can.

In a letter to three Chicago daily newspaper editors following the show, the Dr. Story Defense Committee charged Oprah with "perpetuating a fraud by allowing false statements and half-truths to be presented as fact by women whose allegations were previously rejected as having no credibility whatsoever."

Oprah also repeatedly mentioned an appointment she had scheduled for that afternoon with her gynecologist and after hearing the lurid accounts of the nine Lovell women, stated that she intended to cancel it. That too, did not go unnoticed by the Defense Committee.

"Programs such as Oprah Winfrey's do a monstrous disservice to the medical profession, and her statement that she was cancelling her OB-GYN appointment as the result of what she had heard should be met with a refusal by every doctor in Chicago to treat her," they said.

Oprah was further villified for her reaction to incoming calls. The day before the show, people who wanted to be heard in Dr. Story's defense were told by the producer that if they called precisely at 8:00 a.m., their calls would be accepted.

One person, not a member of the defense committee, was on the line at 8:00 a.m. and spoke to Oprah herself, who said she had a live show to do and was not accepting calls.

Others following were denied access to the program by receptionists. Later on, however, one call was taken from a woman expressing her appreciation for the program. As she spoke to the caller, Oprah struck a dramatic pose, one hand raised as if to receive a final judgment from above.

"It was a suitable finish to a contrived production," the committee noted.

* The group was flown to Chicago and housed in a "posh" hotel at network expense, Terri Timmons told a newspaper reporter on her return, but otherwise, she added piously, they received "no compensation."

"We just wanted to help other women," she said.

CHAPTER 48

Dr. Story's sister, Gretchen Stevens, lives in nearby Wheaton, Illinois and she made it a point to attend the Oprah Winfrey show on the day she knew her brother was to be tried again before television viewers from coast to coast.

She went armed with complete confidence in her brother's innocence and the knowledge that as a Christian, she would not be alone in her efforts to defend him.

What she did not bargain for was Oprah's hostility. As Gretchen tried to point out her brother's stability as a Christian, the possibility of a conspiracy and lack of cooperation from the State, Oprah repeated her words derisively and then turned her back on the resolute little woman. Even so, viewers must have felt that Gretchen gave a good account of herself and Dr. Story's supporters praised her courage in taking on a seasoned show business performer, however useless the effort.

When Gretchen sat down, Oprah turned to Judi Cashel, who showed more compassion than the host of the show, when she conceded that no sister would want to believe that her brother was a rapist. A short review of Judi's own part in the case then got the situation back on track and the show ended with another verdict of "guilty."

CHAPTER 49

In contrast to Oprah Winfrey's one-sided presentation of the Dr. Story case, "60 Minutes" took a more balanced view.

Although clearly designed to arouse curiosity and questions about the conviction of this small-town physician, the "60 Minutes" segment was disappointing to some of his friends, who had hoped for more exposure on the doctor's side of the story.

First, "60 Minutes" producer Norm Gorin and then Morley Safer, plus other investigators and a camera crew, spent several days in Lovell interviewing both the alleged victims and the doctor's wife, daughter Susan and members of the Defense Committee.

Jan Hillman, who appeared briefly on the program, said afterward, "We knew that they were skeptical of the accusers' stories and very sympathetic to us, particularly Doc's family."

That part of the information gathering wasn't included in the final production, however, and Doc's supporters were surprised and a little disappointed.

"The program brought us considerable publicity, though," Jan says now, "and some financial help, so we felt good about it."

Comments came from all over.

"I have never been so ashamed of our

judicial system. It is an outrage." - Massachusetts.

"I can identify with any woman who has been raped - those women were not raped by Dr. Story."- Seattle.

"Not enough anger from any woman who had been raped!" - Iowa.

"'60 Minutes' made me stop and think about the possibility of his being innocent." - New Jersey.

All were encouraging, so the Committee took their disappointment in stride and kept on working.

CHAPTER 50

This time, no one was anonymous. Morley Safer, narrator for the "60 Minutes" segment on March 1, 1987, introduced each of the participating "victims" and even identified the woman who started it all as Arden McArthur, who in his words, "began seeking and mobilizing the doctor's patients."

Safer carefully avoided naming the Mormon church, but did refer to Arden's "religious experience" which prompted her to "do something about Dr. Story." He also noted that the three McArthur women, Arden, Meg and Minda, who had once been "so vocal on the subject of the doctor, now refused to be interviewed."

Mr. Safer did not say, but Lovell residents know, that Arden did attend the first meeting between the accusers and "60 Minutes" investigators and spent the whole time there stroking a half grown cat she brought with her.

The account which was aired began with Wanda Hammond, whose delivery improved with each performance. In court, she had seemed hesitant, on the Oprah Winfrey show her backbone had stiffened somewhat, but by March 1987, she was an old trooper and the words flowed freely. Always on the verge of tears, Wanda's concluding statement, when asked why she hadn't reported the incident which supposedly happened in 1958, was a pitiful, "Who would've believed a (pause) country (pause) lady?"

Safer skillfully brought out the ridiculous. Aletha Durtsche told him, "I went back to Dr. Story (after an absence from Lovell) because I didn't really believe that he had raped me." Deftly, he underscored the unthinkable when Hayla Farwell, under his questioning, admitted that she had allowed her mother to take her children to Dr. Story after the alleged rape.

Master showman that he is, Safer barely suppressed a laugh when 77-year-old Emma Lu Meeks said, when he asked her why a man would risk assaulting a police officer's wife, "Don't ask me! I'm not a flirty person." He then further exposed her incredibility by telling the audience that following the supposed rape attempt, Emma Lu went to the desk and "calmly paid her bill."

Emma Lu, too, had attempted to sharpen up her act and in response to a comment following the Oprah Winfrey show that none of the women were "angry enough" to be true rape victims, she tried valiantly to display the proper indignation.

"That is the most degrading thing that can happen to a person," she said loudly, "to be raped by a - uh uh," at which point a voice in the background prompted, "trusted doctor," and she dutifully repeated the words.

Morley Safer, to the satisfaction of the Defense Committee, persistently wove the Arden McArthur thread through the entire segment. In the final few minutes when Dr. Story himself was interviewed, he was specifically asked about her and the doctor's response was quick and positive as he detailed the difficulties he had with the McArthur family after twenty years of treating them all.

As he appeared with Safer in the visitors' area of the Wyoming state penitentiary, the doctor looked, acted and spoke much as he has always done, and his friends, most of whom have not seen him since his return to the penitentiary, were encouraged.

Knowing his great faith, they took comfort in the fact that the brutal realities of prison had changed him very little. To those who did not know him, he was unconvincing for the same reasons that his friends saw him as unchanged.

Dr. Story's voice and manner, never commanding, did not spark instant enthusiasm for his innocence, but on the other hand, didn't give the impression of guilt, either. He was almost matter-of-fact in his explanation of the events leading to his downfall, until Morley Safer mentioned that the women who had accused their physician of rape had not "deviated" from their stories.

The doctor paused and then said, "Um, what happens to them if they do deviate, if they do back out on their accusations?" to which Safer replied, "Well, they're religious women - their souls will be saved."

Dr. Story gave a characteristic half-laugh. "Pretty simple," he said, "and they'd be liable for some kind of prosecution, wouldn't they?"

If that question was answered, it was left on the cutting room floor, because Safer's next comment was that people watching the program were likely to say, "he's got to be guilty, because he's not angry enough." Anger again. Victims should be angry - an innocent man should be angry. Dr. Story responded with the nearest thing to anger his friends and family had ever seen him display in public.

"And you apparently don't see that anger, do you?" he said, and then, "I wish you could see it here (pointing to his heart) instead of up here (touching his head), but then he lapsed into his usual equivocal manner of expressing himself.

" My anger is not in me all the time - it comes and goes," he said, "and how am I handling it? How do you handle something you have no control over?"

To an audience hoping for a forceful statement from a man serving an unjust sentence, this fell flat and the next day, when asked what they thought of the program, his supporters had to say, as they had following the trial, "Doc didn't do himself any good."

As for the accusers, they came across as women whose stories at best were questionable, but the fact remains - they are free and Dr. Story is in prison.

CHAPTER 51

The relationships of Dr. Story's accusers to one another, to the Lovell Police Department, and to other principals in the case are among the most significant aspects to be considered in any study of the Story conviction.

The original accusers were Meg and Minda McArthur, represented by their mother, Arden Tanner McArthur.

Meg McArthur is married to Daniel Anderson, who with his mother, Dorcus Anderson, is employed by the Lovell Police Department.

Minda McArthur is married to Scott Brinkerhoff, whose mother, Dorothy, was another accuser. Dorothy was not a prosecution witness in Dr. Story's criminal trial, but was included with the complaining witnesses in their public appearances after the conviction. Dorothy and Dorcus Anderson are sisters and Dorothy's son-in-law, Frankie Rohrer, is also employed by the Lovell Police Department.

Minda is also a niece by marriage to LaVelle Brinkerhoff, a state investigator at the time of the McArthurs' accusations.

LaVelle is a half-brother to Gerald Brinkerhoff, Minda's father-in-law and former business partner with Dr. Story. Gerald testified for the prosecution and

LaVelle was in the Big Horn Basin area during the trial.

Hayla Farwell, a complaining witness, is related to two members of the Lovell Police Department staff - her brother, Jon Fink, and Geneveive Fink, her aunt.

Wanda Hammond is closely related to another non-charging accuser and Frank Florez, a Lovell police officer, was related by marriage to still another non-charging accuser.

Carol Peterson, a complaining witness, is the daughter of Pam Mayer, a disgruntled former employee of Dr. Story's who testified for the prosecution. Pam was later employed by Dr. John Welch, another Lovell physician.

Aletha Durtsche and Annella St. Thomas, both complaining witnesses, are cousins.

Emma Lu Meeks, complaining witness, is an aunt by marriage to Diana Harrison, former Story employee who testified against him at the criminal trial. Diana also went to work for Dr. John Welch later. Emma Lu's husband was a Lovell police officer at the time of the alleged assault.

Gertrude Jolley, complaining witness, is Emma Lu's cousin, best friend and neighbor. Gertrude's granddaughter, Jacque Wagner, is employed by the Lovell Police Department.

Terri Timmons, complaining witness, is a cousin to Meg Anderson and Minda Brinkerhoff.

Most of the women who testified against Dr. Story were related to one another or to the McArthur family or both, and more than half of them have one or more connections with the Lovell Police Department.

CHAPTER 52

Dr. Story's attorneys, Mason and Graham, were tenacious. After Dr. Story's return to prison, their next step was to submit a federal appeal (Writ of Certiorari) to the U.S. Supreme Court in October 1986, but in January 1987, it was learned that this too, was unsuccessful. With two thousand to choose from, only two hundred Writs were selected for consideration during that term and the Lovell doctor's was not one of them.

The Defense Committee's January 1987 issue of "The Real Story" reported that "it now appears the most potential lies in pursuing our cause through the Federal District Court with the possibility of appeal to the Tenth Circuit in Denver. Dr. Story will be making this decision soon."

Back in jail after the failure of his appeal to the Wyoming Supreme Court, John H. Story, M.D. soon found that he had the means and time to not only keep his mind active, but add to his knowledge of the law, which admittedly at that point, was almost nil.

With his keen mind and tough determination, he approached the study of law as he had his first love, medicine. With the help of a sophisticated typewriter purchased for him by a group of his friends, in less than a year he was, to no one's surprise, ready to take charge of his own defense.

Actually, even to his attorneys, this seemed the logical way to go, since the doctor had, from the beginning, insisted that all efforts in his behalf, legal and otherwise, be channeled through and controlled by him. Any effort to bypass him was met with a sharp rebuke. Further, with legal expenses sky rocketing and both the Storys' finances and the Defense Committee's funds depleted, a pro se approach seemed reasonable and was accepted by the Court.

In the meantime, however, legal maneuverings were continuing through 1987 with attorneys Mason and Graham filing a motion with the lower court for a new trial on grounds of new evidence. This was based on the alleged perjury of Wanda Hammond in the criminal trial, when she denied ever having an IUD placed by Dr. Story.*

The petition was accompanied by an affidavit by Parthena Thompson, Wanda's sister-in-law, who stated that Wanda told her when the IUD was inserted. The motion also stated that Dr. Ray Christensen of Powell, Wyoming (by then deceased) had removed the IUD before performing a hysterectomy on Wanda and that his records would confirm that fact.

Also included in the motion was the statement that because the jury believed Wanda's false statement rather than the notation on her medical record, they believed the doctor to be lying and that he falsified his records, a perception which carried over to the other witnesses' charges.

"Unperjured testimony by Hammond," it read,"...could have resulted in 'not guilty' verdicts on all six counts of which the defendant was convicted."

Prosecuting Attorney Tharp, understandably, received this motion with little enthusiasm. He warned that the motion would "likely" go before Judge Gary Hartman, who presided over the trial in 1985.

"The judge can either decide to hear the evidence and thus schedule a hearing, or dismiss the motion summarily," he said and added that if a hearing were held, the judge would then make the decision if there would be a new trial or not.

Despite this explanation, in a news story in the Billings Gazette on August 19, 1987, Tharp, not the judge, made the announcement that the motion had been automatically denied because the defense attorney didn't ask for a determination within ten days after it was filed, a technicality which was soon to be challenged.

In September, it became official - the judge had, for the exact reason stated by Tharp in his news release, denied the motion for a new trial and in so doing, denied the necessity for investigating the charge of perjury. This obvious "ex parte (in the interest of one side only) communication" between prosecutor and judge was also to become the subject of a later appeal.

Again, letters flooded the Big Horn County court house, urging Tharp to pursue the charge of perjury on the part of Wanda Hammond with as much diligence as he had pursued the charges against Dr. Story. Mr. Tharp didn't do so.

The manner in which the matter had been handled, though, cried out for further action and Doc, from prison, immediately began an appeal of that denial. He filed it with the Wyoming Supreme Court on November 19, 1987 and succeeded in getting it on the expedited docket. Maybe at last, he had gotten the State's attention.

Meanwhile, back in Lovell, Jan Hillman and Wes Meeker had been doing their homework. They knew from reading the Wyoming Statutes that county commissioners can request a special prosecutor from the Attorney General's office upon failure or refusal of the county attorney to act in any criminal case. Armed with affidavits and other written proof of perjury, they went to see their Big Horn County Commissioners.

What happened to that effort was described in the next Defense Committee newsletter:

"They (Jan and Wes) asked for a special prosecutor to be appointed, and presented to the commissioners letters and responses from County Prosecuting Attorney Terrill Tharp, showing his prejudice in this case. Two of the commissioners were responsive at first, but the third, Ken Bullinger, said he didn't think they should get involved. All of them agreed they would discuss it and let us (the committee) know."

On November 6, 1987, the Defense Committee received a letter from County Commissioners Chairman James Rannells, saying they had discussed the matter with Scott McColloch, assistant county attorney under Terrill Tharp, and that he had advised the Board to get the request in writing. The Defense Committee complied.

Just a month later, the newsletter continued, the Committee received another letter, this time from Scott McColloch, in which he stated that the county commissioners had met with Terry Tharp concerning their request for a special prosecutor.

"After discussing the matter with Mr. Tharp," he wrote, "the county commissioners feel that he has acted on this matter within the scope of the county attorney's discretion. Therefore, the county commissioners have denied your request for a special prosecutor."

"No one questioned that Tharp acted within his scope of discretion," Jan said later. "We questioned only his vision, totally prejudiced and blind regarding this case. He can't possibly be fair when the matter involves the biggest 'win' of his career. He is also not about to question the veracity of one of his prize witnesses, because if he did, he would have to question the entire case against Dr. Story, which he prosecuted."

* This was one of the unexplainable actions taken by the prosecution and allowed by the judge in Dr. Story's criminal trial. Throughout, witnesses were allowed to choose dates from their physician's confiscated charts as the day of the alleged assaults and change dates to coincide with their last visits to Dr. Story. But when the defense attempted to use the same documents to show the reason for a visit or that no pelvic examination was performed on a particular day in question, it was implied that the doctor falsified his records!

"For the first time in too long, we have received good news concerning Dr. Story's case!" Defense Committee

CHAPTER 53

"A lower court erred when it failed to consider the merits of a motion filed by Lovell physician, Dr. John H. Story," the Powell Tribune, a semi-weekly newspaper in the Big Horn Basin, reported May 24, 1988.

The front-page article went on to say that the unanimous decision of the Supreme Court was that Dr. Story was entitled to a hearing on his motion for a new trial.

"A court abuses its discretion when it acts in a manner which exceeds the bounds of reason under the circumstances," they said, and Justice Walter Urbigkit wrote a special concurrence.

"Not only do I find that a hearing is required," Judge Urbigkit wrote, "but a hearing **with live testimony**, where the facts will be established before the decision on a motion for new trial...is made." (emphasis added)

Justice Urbigkit concluded with a personal reference to his own "deepfelt anguish" about any possibility of perjury in a criminal conviction.

The Storys and their supporters were jubilant. Surely with a decision like this from the high court, Judge Hartman could not so easily dismss their request! Wrong again.

Immediately following the Supreme

Court's decision, Dr. Story resumed his legal stratagems from prison. For one, he decided that outside criminal defense representation was again necessary and began a search for the right attorney.

"We have learned there is no justice when contending against the State without a commitment to aggressive representation," he said, and by July had retained Irvin B. Nodland and Thomas A. Dickson from Bismarck, North Dakota.

In August, new motions were filed with the lower court. One was to obtain depositions and to subpoena some important records which would prove perjury on the part of one of the accusers, and the other was to disqualify Judge Hartman from further action in the case.

On October 5, 1988, a hearing was held in Judge Hartman's court and the motion to disqualify himself was denied.

On November 14, 1988, another hearing was held in Judge Hartman's court, this time on the motion for "opportunity to take depositions," but under rather strange circumstances.

Dr. Story's lawyers, Irvin Nodland and Tom Dickson, had been trying since their entry into the case to be granted an evidentiary hearing before Judge Hartman, to no avail.

Since they had heard nothing to indicate that the November 14th proceedings would be any more than just a hearing of arguments by the judge, they made no preparation for witnesses to appear.

On the evening of November 13, Marilyn Story and some of her friends decided they would at least attend the hearing just to see what was going on. They contacted Attorney Dick Kahl in Powell, who had done some work for Nodland and Dickson and the next morning they were all on their way to Basin.

The current appeal by Dr. Story to the Supreme Court states simply,"At this hearing the prosecution was permitted to produce witness testimony for the record; the judge called and questioned witnesses; the defense was not provided notice and was therefore, inadequately prepared."

The Defense Committee, in its next issue of the "Real Story" was more emotional in its description.

"As we walked into the court house," it read, "we were very surprised to find about twenty accusers or friends of accusers, plus subpoenaed witnesses from Lovell and Powell ready to testify against Dr. Story and Marilyn."

Apparently, it continued, the prosecution and the judge had a "mini-trial" all prepared without having notified the defense attorneys that it would be a hearing with live evidence.

Attorney Dickson said later, "if we had known there was to be live evidence allowed, we would certainly have been there with our witnesses, as that was exactly what we had been hoping for."

The item in the Defense Committee newsletter concluded with, "it shouldn't surprise us, but it still does."

Mr. Kahl was able to argue for Dr. Story, but under the disadvantage of not being adequately prepared.

Marilyn, too, was unexpectedly called to the stand to describe her successful effort to obtain information from the office of the Powell doctor who was believed to have removed Wanda Hammond's IUD.

"Tharp tried to make me look like a criminal for looking at the record," she said later. "He claimed that I had copied the record, which I denied. He said, 'Mrs. Story, what would you say if I told you that someone saw you copy the record?' and I said 'I would say that they are liars, because I did not copy the record.'"

Since that time, three affidavits have been received from former nurses and office employees of Dr. Christensen, confirming the information Marilyn Story saw regarding Wanda's IUD.

After the hearing, Kay Holm, in her usual forthright way, challenged Tharp to bring perjury charges against Wanda Hammond, but his answer was, "it is really confusing," and "it is now in the judge's hands."

In December, a Lovell native, Burt Huntington, well known in the Big Horn Basin as the sharp-tongued editor of the Lovell Chronicle for sixteen years, wrote to the editor of that publication from his present home in Red Lodge, Montana.

Recalling his early years in Lovell, Huntington said, "I don't need a program since I know most of the players."

Although politically, Doc and Burt were exact opposites and had many lively, sometimes heated discussions, Burt described his old antagonist as having a "keen analytical mind and logical thought processes."

Unfortunately," he continued, "Doc also thought there is a basic human goodness in each individual. That, coupled with his being an independent thinker, is no doubt what made it so easy to railroad him into prison."

"Now that there is new evidence that should be brought to light in the cause of justice," Huntington continued, "it appears that both the judge and prosecuting attorney are doing their best to keep it swept under the rug. Why wouldn't they want the truth to be known? Makes one wonder just how far the plot extends."

Burt Huntington isn't proud of his home town of Lovell any more, he says, but still has hope that the "real and complete truth will some day be known."

Two months later, on January 31, 1989, Judge Gary Hartman handed down his decision denying Dr. Story a new trial, and simultaneously denying the motion to take depositions to support evidence demanding that new trial.

At least one Story supporter wrote to Justice Urbigkit asking if the hearing in the lower court and the manner in which it was conducted was what he and his fellow justices intended.

There was no answer.

CHAPTER 54

There are still loose ends to be tied, one by one, in the strange case of a harmless Christian physician who found himself in the center of a whirlwind of lies, distortions and incongruities.

Since Dr. Story's latest appeal was filed, much publicity has been given the case, most of it editorial comment.

One accusation which has surfaced against "the establishment" is that there were reports made to authorities at the time of the alleged rapes, but were ignored.

Here is the information gleaned from official records:

Two women who testified against Dr. Story in his criminal trial claimed to have made complaints about him to some authority.

(1) Annella St. Thomas said that she told her husband two weeks later about the alleged assault in Dr. Story's office.

Nelson St. Thomas said he talked to then Police Chief LaMar Averett, who said in court that he took no action, **because there was no evidence.**

The St. Thomases, according to court testimony, then wrote a letter to the State Board of Medical Examiners and received a reply stating that the Board already had one complaint against Dr. Story.

Here the assertion broke down, however, because in a pre-trial statement taken by Judi Cashel, Mr. St. Thomas said the Board replied by saying "they would need more corroborative evidence before they could proceed."

The St. Thomases could produce no letter to substantiate either of these claims and the State Medical Board denied ever receiving their letter. This denial can hardly be disputed, considering the immediate attention given the letters written to the Board later by Meg Anderson and Minda Brinkerhoff.

(2) Carol Peterson allegedly told her mother, Pam Mayer, about her experience with Dr. Story and Pam then told her husband and Carol's father, Walt Mayer, about it.

In court, Walt said that he called Dee Cozzens, then hospital administrator in Lovell and asked him to set up an appointment with the doctor.

The meeting was arranged and Mr. Mayer testified that he asked Dr. Story "about what my wife had told me," and added, "he denied it.

The former Bishop in the LDS church then stated that Dr. Story had told him that he (Dr. Story) had "left himself open for that kind of a charge (by) not having someone in the room." and that the doctor said he would take care of the matter by having a nurse present during examinations.

During cross-examination, Mr. Mayer was asked, "So far as you are concerned, the matter was laid to rest as a result of that meeting?" and Mr. Mayer answered, "That's correct."

Former Hospital Administrator Dee Cozzens also testified, but his statements could hardly be considered proof of anything.

He was not present at the meeting, he said, and described Mr. Mayer's request as being because "he had some concern about something that apparently happened at Dr. Story's office."

"Did he go into details surrounding the complaint?" the prosecuting attorney asked, and Dee replied, "No, he did not."

He later reiterated this, saying, "the details of what happened were not given to me other than the fact that something had occurred at the office."

Following Dr. Story's meeting with Mr. Mayer, Cozzens said he suggested to the doctor that "to avoid any problems" there should be a female person in the examining room with him when he did a female examination.

In this case, both the complaint and the reaction to it appear so mild as to have been almost non-existent.

One other report allegedly made to an authority in Lovell was by the McArthur sisters, Meg and Minda, who stated that in 1983 they went to their bishop, Larry Sessions, with their story of alleged "violations" by Dr. Story. He surprised them, they said, by saying he had been hearing similar accusations for five years.

If the bishop actually made that comment, he put himself in an awkward position as a husband and leader in the church, because his wife was a patient of Dr. Story's and continued to be until after September 1983, when he performed major surgery on her.

Mr. Sessions made no formal denial of

the comment he was said to have made, but did try later to discourage his fellow church members from taking any action against the doctor.

* * *

After the trial, word got out that one woman juror was very upset over the verdict. This prompted the Dr. Story Defense Committee to interview as many of the jurors as possible and they made some interesting discoveries before Judge Hartman issued a letter suggesting to jurors that conversations with defense committee members might be of a critical nature. (Taped interviews show that this was not the case - they were conducted with dignity and compassion and the jurors responded in like manner.)

It was learned that during deliberations, there were matters discussed which were prejudicial to Dr. Story. For instance, Meg and Minda's original accusations and the lawsuits they had filed against the doctor were talked about and questions raised as to why they and other accusers were not a part of the criminal case. This was in direct opposition to the care taken by both prosecution and defense during the trial to avoid any mention of the Medical Board hearing or its outcome.

Further, jurors said they had perused the medical records and if the doctor's writing was "sketchy" or "didn't explain what he did," they "tended to find him guilty" in those cases. Susan Story, who had by then been working as a registered nurse for six years, was indignant that people outside of the medical profession, regardless of their intelligence or education in other fields, would presume to judge a doctor by his patient charting.

One woman juror claimed during deliberations to have had intimate relations with her attorney in his office while his wife was working nearby, thus probably reinforcing the allegation that Marilyn and Dr. Story's employees could have been unaware of rape going on in the examining room.

No juror would infer that a mistake could have been made, but at least one seemed genuinely uneasy about her role as a decision maker in the Dr. Story case.

* * *

Adverse testimony was accepted from a person whose relationship with Dr. Story had reached such a point of bitterness that it is difficult to see how it could be objective.

Pam Mayer, who had worked for the doctor for less than three months, made frequent references in her pre-trial investigative reports to the animosity she felt toward her former employer.

"He would lecture me for an hour," she said repeatedly about the doctor's reaction to mistakes she had made, and "you always felt like you were on a tightrope and were going to do something wrong."

In spite of the fact that Mrs. Mayer admitted under oath that she left Dr. Story's employ because "it was obvious I didn't understand the rules in his office," she was allowed to describe in full what Mr. Tharp had referred to in pre-trial questioning as Dr. Story's "weird practices."

Although they consisted mainly of guidelines the doctor expected his employees to follow in dealing with patients in general, and pertained to none of the complaining witnesses, these "revelations" were given an important place in the prosecution's rebuttal, and Dr. Story had no opportunity to comment on them.

* * *

Then there is the matter of Mormon women.

Lovell women, with the implication that the Mormon Church has total control over their minds and lifestyles, were portrayed by Judi Cashel as being "raised to be victims."

Describing them further, she insisted that they were totally subservient to men and therefore the perfect targets for "power rape."

This was an opinion not backed by facts. Anyone who has lived among Mormons knows that there are LDS women who are completely family-oriented, as are some Lutherans, Baptists and Catholics, but this does not make them weak-willed, and many dominate their large families.

Just as in any other community, there are Mormon women who work outside the home and they take pride in their abilities.

They are not "women's libbers" - the Church frowns on that - but they unhesitatingly do what must be done to help support the family or fulfill their own needs. Those who are not employed otherwise, are willing, even eager, to take on leadership roles in church, clubs and civic activities.

Mormon women, particularly mothers, are extremely conscious of the advantages of education and are often the driving force in getting their children through college by whatever means possible.

Emma Lu Meeks, though small, could hardly be said to be intimidated by anyone - even her policeman husband - and Terri Timmons, at the other end of the age spectrum, is anything but a submissive woman.

While all of the nine complaining witnesses against Dr. Story, Mormon or otherwise, were, in the opinion of other Lovell residents, susceptible to suggestion and prone to mass hysteria, to label them (and by inference their Mormon sisters) "raised to be victims," is a generality which can't be proved.

* * *

The women involved in the Dr. Story case had probably never heard the term "power rape," until after they made their allegations against their doctor and were consequently enrolled in counselling by a woman operating out of the Big Horn County Behavioral Center, Patricia Wiseman.

Here they learned the satisfactions of group therapy and spent many hours rehashing the accusations they had made and would continue to make even after Dr. Story was locked away. Their later claims that they had suffered emotional havoc during the years between the alleged assaults and their accusations were thought by many who knew them to be nothing more than reaction to counselling, since there had never been the slightest hint to relatives, close friends or neighbors that they had suffered any abuse by their family physician.

In Lovell, the slightest deviation from the norm is immediately and avidly noticed, and to believe that continuing sexual assaults would never surface in seventeen years, is not consistent with the town's reputation.

Further, the accusers' court testimony, in comparison with pre-trial statements, had been carefully groomed and polished, with the most unbelievable portions deleted or changed for improved credibility.

Who then, outside of Lovell, cared so much about bringing down a man whose life reflected only the determination to be a good doctor, a good family man and a good witness for Christianity?

Wayne Aarestad, in his closing argument, asked the jury to ponder this question.

"As you weigh the testimony of these women," he said, " you are going to get this picture. **THE TRUTH IS GOING TO EMERGE** as to what this case is all about. And what you will see is that somebody either wants Dr. Story out of Lovell or wants him out of practice, but is out to get him."

THE TRUTH WILL EMERGE. That is what keeps Dr. Story, his family, his friends and the many supporters he has gained over the past four years, working and praying for eventual justice.

EPILOGUE

When I was a young woman, pregnant with my first child, I was in my yard one summer day when a hit-and-run driver struck a neighborhood dog. The animal seemed to be more stunned than injured, but as he tried to get up, another dog came from nowhere, it seemed, and attacked him. To my horror, another and yet another appeared, until the street was alive with snarling, biting animals.

Forgetting my condition, I ran screaming and flailing my arms toward the writhing mass. As I drew closer, though, I saw the blood and heard the fierce sounds as the attackers swarmed mercilessly over their victim and I knew there was nothing I could do to stop them.

In tears, my heavy body aching from exertion, heart beating wildly, I hurried home where I watched with loathing until the assailants tired of the game and ran away, playfully nipping and barking at one another.

The victim, now badly hurt, lay quietly for a few seconds, then dragged his torn body to the shelter of some bushes, where he collapsed again.

My son arrived the next day and in the excitement of new motherhood, I never found out what happened to the injured dog. I can still remember, though, the cold, helpless feeling I had as I watched that poor animal set upon by his friends of the day before, when they all played together on the green lawns of a quiet neighborhood.

I am a grandmother now, and I have seen a relentless attack upon an innocent man. And I wonder, as did Solomon in Ecclesiastes 3:21, "Who knoweth the spirit of man that goeth upward and the spirit of the beast that goeth down to the earth?"

Jeane S. Wagner

ABOUT THE AUTHOR

"Without Evidence, The Rape of Justice in Wyoming," is Jeane Wagner's first book, but she has been writing "forever."

"My first published work was a letter to the editor of the Rocky Mountain News in Denver, written at the age of eight," she says, "and from then on, I was hooked."

From a reporter, columnist and feature writer for the Lovell Chronicle in Lovell, Wyoming, Jeane went to freelancing, and had news and feature articles published in Parade Magazine, The American Rose, The Billings Gazette, Casper Star Tribune, and other Wyoming newspapers, winning a Wyoming Press Association Pacemaker Award for "Best News Story."

During the 70's, her writing consisted of brochures, speeches and advertising for several political campaigns, and promotional writing for the Big Horn Basin area.

In 1976, with their children grown, Jeane and her husband, Chuck, moved to Wyoming's capital city, where she worked for an elected official, composing and editing news releases among other duties until 1989.

In 1986, with an old friend in the penitentiary for crimes he didn't commit, Jeane started using her spare time to write a book on what no one wants to believe - that an innocent man can go to prison.

"Without Evidence" is the result of those three years of research and writing.

Today Mrs. Wagner lives in Cheyenne with her husband, happily surrounded by a daughter and her family, a son, her mother, a flower garden and a little white cat.

And that's the way she likes it.